the popcorn principles

A NOVELIST'S GUIDE TO LEARNING FROM MOVIES

JOHN GASPARD

The Popcorn Principles: A Novelist's Guide To Learning From Movies

First Edition | February 2023

https://www.albertsbridgebooks.com

All rights reserved. No part of this book may be used or reproduced in any manner whatsoever, including Internet usage, without written permission from the author, except in the case of brief quotations embodied in critical articles and reviews.

Unless otherwise listed in the Notes section, all quotes are taken from interviews the author conducted for the books *"Fast Cheap and Under Control,"* *"Fast Cheap and Written That Way,"* *"Tell Them It's a Dream Sequence,"* and *"Women Make Movies."*

CONTENTS

Introduction   v

PART ONE
PRE-PRODUCTION

PRINCIPLE #1   3
STOP GETTING READY AND JUST DO IT

PRINCIPLE #2   8
READ. WRITE. REPEAT

PRINCIPLE #3   11
EXPLOIT THE UNIQUE

PRINCIPLE #4   17
STAY IN YOUR LANE

PRINCIPLE #5   21
YOU GOTTA BE COMMITTED

PART TWO
PRODUCTION

PRINCIPLE #6   29
COME IN LATE, LEAVE EARLY

PRINCIPLE #7   34
CUTTING THE SHOE LEATHER

PRINCIPLE #8   39
INTENTIONS & OBSTACLES

PRINCIPLE #9   42
DON'T SPILL ALL YOUR POPCORN IN THE LOBBY (GIVE YOUR CHARACTERS A SECRET)

PRINCIPLE #10   46
SAVE THE CAT, KILL THE CAT. I DON'T CARE. JUST CREATE AN EMOTIONAL CONNECTION

PRINCIPLE #11   50
CALLBACKS — DON'T FORGET TO REAP WHAT YOU SOW

PRINCIPLE #12   55
GREAT EXPOSITION DOESN'T SOUND LIKE EXPOSITION

PRINCIPLE #13   62
THEATER OF THE MINIMAL

PRINCIPLE #14 *KEEP LESTER AWAKE*	66
PRINCIPLE #15 *ALL'S WELL THAT ENDS WELL*	69

PART THREE
POST-PRODUCTION

PRINCIPLE #16 *PREVIEWS!*	77
PRINCIPLE #17 *GETTING NOTES*	83
PRINCIPLE #18 *THERE IS NO SHAME IN RESHOOTING*	88
PRINCIPLE #19 *KILL YOUR DARLINGS*	94
PRINCIPLE #20 *DON'T HESITATE TO HESITATE*	102

PART FOUR
DISTRIBUTION

PRINCIPLE #21 *READ THE FINE PRINT*	109
PRINCIPLE #22 *HIGH FIVES & HARSH WORDS: THE REVIEWS ARE IN*	116
PRINCIPLE #23 *NEVER NEED HOLLYWOOD*	119
PRINCIPLE #24 *TIME IS ON YOUR SIDE*	124
PRINCIPLE #25 *THE BEST ADVICE*	129
Afterword	131
Get Your Free Eli Marks Short Story Bundle	133
Get Your Free Como Lake Players Short Mystery	135
Join The Newsletter	137
About the Author	139
Books By John Gaspard	141
NOTES	143
FILMOGRAPHY	152

INTRODUCTION

"Oh, that's just a popcorn movie."

How often has that phrase been uttered in what was, probably, a slightly derisive manner?

Too often, if you ask me.

The fact is that most of these so-called "popcorn movies" usually demonstrate outstanding storytelling skills, muscles which they flex with ease throughout their various running times. Much can be learned by observing the principles at work in these seemingly effortless confections.

So, what does that have to do with how you go about writing your own fiction?

It could be a lot.

Conventional wisdom suggests the best way to write a great novel is to read other great novels. Which is true. *(Look no further than Principle #2 in this book.)*

Up to a point.

However, while reading a great work of fiction—like watching a classic magic routine—it's often impossible to see how the trick is being done. You instinctively know they've done *something* amazing, but for the life of you, you can't figure out how they pulled it off.

Sometimes it's easier to recognize and absorb the tricks of storytelling in a *different* medium, and then adapt those ideas into your writing.

There is—admittedly—a world of difference between making movies and writing novels. However, there are some areas which definitely overlap. Outstanding books and movies engage audiences by telling compelling, involving stories.

The best, most crowd-pleasing films—sometimes called popcorn movies—do this by employing some key concepts, which, as it turns out, are there for the taking by novelists.

These are what I call The Popcorn Principles.

Twenty-five precepts, gleaned from all phases of the motion picture creation process (Pre-Production, Production, Post-Production and Distribution). As you'll see, there is surprising overlap between what they do and the process of creating, refining and releasing books.

That's the meaning behind the book's title and its subtitle, and the goal of this slim volume: To help you see how the illusion is being pulled off in movies, inspiring you to create your own versions of these tricks in the books and stories you write.

But first a little background.

I've written and produced a half-dozen low-budget feature films. Along the way, I've written several books on film production. These books are filled with tips and workarounds for beginners, taken from interviews I've had with more than a hundred filmmakers.

In the process of writing those books, I had the privilege of talking to some of the industry's top filmmakers.

Like producer (and legend) Roger Corman.

Or directors, such as Steven Soderbergh, Jon Favreau, Stuart

Gordon, Kasi Lemmons, Lesli Linka Glater, George Romero, Bob Clark, and Miranda July.

And screenwriters, like Kenneth Lonergan (Academy Award winner), Dan Futterman and Whit Stillman (both nominated for Academy Awards), Dan O'Bannon, Susan Coyne, and Rebecca Miller.

And editors, such as Roger Nygard, Dody Dorn and Carol Littleton.

And even a handful of terrific actors, like Edie Falco, Mo Collins, Alan Cumming, Barbara Steele, Griffin Dunne and Tom Noonan (who, by the way, would also fit comfortably into any of the previous categories—producer, director, writer and editor).

I used the tips they offered (on all aspects of filmmaking) to craft four books for beginning filmmakers, giving them tips on how to succeed and get their movies made.

Then I started writing novels (over a dozen of them as of this writing), and a funny thing happened: I came to realize that many of the filmmaking principles the pros had given me worked in my fiction writing as well.

Not all of them, of course. Some were too technical in nature and referred to aspects which were unique to the world of filmmaking.

But many of the principles not only applied to writing fiction, but also were a great help in making my writing better.

Several of the best principles came (not so surprisingly) from the screenwriters I spoke to. The construction of a screenplay for a movie is often a master class in compression, in which each and every element is designed to move the story on a forward trajectory. Each moment leads (both inevitably and surprisingly) to the next dramatic moment.

But it wasn't just the screenwriters. The directors, the producers, the editors, even the actors offered great ideas which could be easily adapted, helping me improve my fiction writing. All I had to do was see how that idea in their world (filmmaking) might fit into my new world (writing novels).

I simply had to look at the idea and ask myself, "What's my version of this?"

What are they doing that I can adapt to my situation?

What spin can I put on their technique to make it my own and improve my story?

How can the way they solved that structural problem help me in structuring my novel?

I believe novelists can learn from the storytelling principles of filmmakers to improve their own writing, simply because I do it every day.

For every book.

And, in the process, it's helped me create stronger, more emotionally involving stories.

What follows are twenty-five principles for you to consider as you sit down to write your next (or current) novel.

Some ideas will speak to you. Others may not. Take what works for you and leave the rest.

These principles are not cliches and tropes—movies and fiction have their own abundant share of those. Instead, what follows are some nuts & bolts ideas that span genres and media but offer value in creating and improving your storytelling process.

I've also included some homework at the end of each chapter: Questions you should ask yourself about your book and how that particular principle might work for you. In addition, I've offered some movie watching assignments, where you can experience the principles expressed in that chapter. (Or just watch some really great movies.)

However, I hope your learning doesn't stop here, within the pages of this book.

Keep your eyes and your mind open. You may also discover

your own connections and ideas as you ingest other media—principles that can help you on your personal novel-writing journey. If you find more, by all means let me know about them!

Until then, grab some popcorn, sit back, and settle in.

We're headed to the movies.

PART ONE
PRE-PRODUCTION

Some key things to think about BEFORE you start writing ...

PRINCIPLE #1
STOP GETTING READY AND JUST DO IT

"You cannot 'try' to write. You either do it or you don't."

IN THE WORLD OF MOVIES, many would-be filmmakers often spend way too much time *getting ready* to make a movie, when they should just be getting out there and doing it. They buy books, read interviews, listen to podcasts, and attend seminar after seminar, spending (and sometimes wasting) precious time (and money) which could be spent creating their projects.

Sound familiar?

The same is often true of fiction writers. Many of us spend months (or years) doing everything *but* write our fiction. We're getting ready to try to do it.

But as Yoda taught us, "There is no 'try,' there is only 'do.'"

Filmmaker Tom Noonan (*What Happened Was…*, *Wifey*) had strong feelings about this sort of active inactivity.

"To 'try' is to struggle in a powerless situation," Noonan explained. "You can 'try' as an actor to get a part in a movie—the ultimate decision is not yours. But you cannot 'try' to write a script. You either do it or you don't. If you have a story you need to tell, then please do what you have to do to tell it. If you have something to say, just say it, whether it's ugly or pretty or wrong or stupid. If you need to do it, please do!"

While it may seem against my best interests to state this so early in this book, many of us fritter away too much time getting ready (with books, and seminars and agonizing over which software to use), when we should be taking action.

It's often better to (as the Nike ads suggest) just do it.

Filmmaker Kevin Smith famously quit film school when he learned the curriculum included everything but making a movie.

"I went for hands-on, technical stuff," Smith remembered. "They were like, 'It's all practice, all practical. No theory.' And then we got there and did theory for three months. So I said, 'Fuck it, I don't need some Canadian dude telling me what Demme was trying to say with *Silence of the Lambs.*'"

He asked for a refund, took the money, and made *Clerks*.

Similarly, filmmaker Robert Rodriguez didn't spend money on books and seminars. Instead, he made money by taking part in a month-long medical experiment. And as soon as he was back home, he dived into production on his no-budget classic, *El Mariachi*.

"I was inventing my own film school," Rodriguez said, "where I would be the only student and where experiences, mistakes, problems, and solutions would be my teachers."

The same was true of writer/director Amy Holden Jones, who didn't wait to be asked to direct a movie. Instead, she took a different route on her path to becoming a director.

"I had never written anything, so I was looking for an

existing script. I went into [Roger Corman's] library of scripts, scripts that he hadn't made, and I took several of them," she told me. "I read one called *Don't Open the Door* by Rita Mae Brown. And it had a prolog that was about eight pages long. It had a dialog scene, a suspense scene and an action scene. I got short ends [leftover film] from shooting projects—my husband was a cinematographer. My neighbor was a soundman. We borrowed some lights, used our own house. I did the special effects, and I got UCLA theater students to act in it.

"We spent three days and shot those first eight pages. Then I dropped off this nine-minute reel for Roger that had a dialog scene, a suspense scene and an action/horror scene, to show him that I could do those three different kinds of things which make up an exploitation movie.

"He called me up and asked me how much it had cost me to do it. And I said it cost about $2,000, which is what it had cost. He said, 'You have a future in the business,' and asked me how much I would need to direct the rest of the script. The truth was, I had never read the rest of the script. All I had read was the first eight pages. So, I just, out of the air, said '$200,000.' And he said, 'Let's do it. You're directing this movie.'"

It's all about taking action. Not waiting for the perfect moment to start writing. But just starting. Because the truth is, there is no perfect moment to start. And there never will be.

You've probably heard the old Chinese proverb, which so succinctly put it this way: *"The best time to plant a tree was 20 years ago. The second-best time is now."*

As Smith, Rodriguez and Holden Jones proved, don't wait for permission to start writing your book.

Just start.

On a related note, when it comes to writing software, I agree with Alex Cox (screenwriter, director, *Repo Man*), who said, "Don't waste your money on software. If you can't set two tabs and remember to capitalize character names, find an easier job—actor, or producer."

Alex went on to say, "Pay no attention to screenwriting books or seminars. They are as useless as screenwriting software."

(In the interest of full transparency, I will admit that this book is being written in Scrivener, a dandy writing program which I'm experimenting with. But all my novels and filmmaking books before this? Each one was typed out in plain old Microsoft Word, which was all I needed to get the job done.)

It's surprisingly easy to become addicted to studying writing (i.e., buying books, listening to podcasts, and going to seminars) at the expense of actually sitting down and writing.

There is certainly value in reading a couple books on the topic of writing (two to consider: Stephen King's *On Writing* and Anne Lamott's *Bird By Bird*).

And it can't hurt to take in a seminar or two (where you will likely get as much or more out of the networking than the presentations) or an on-line course (in that area, Mark Dawson's *Self-Publishing Launchpad* is worth considering).

But after that, stop spending money on learning resources and get down to the real learning. You'll do that by writing draft after draft.

I recently came across this in a fortune cookie: *"Even if you're on the right track, you'll get run over if you just sit there."*

With writing, as with many things, one learns best by doing.

So, start doing.

BEYOND THE SCREEN QUESTIONS

- What's stopping you from starting?
- What's one step you can take right now to get started on your book?

- What's the worst thing that could happen if you just started?
- What's your version of what Smith, Rodriguez and Holden-Jones did to kickstart their careers?

Film Suggestions

Clerks

El Mariachi

Repo Man

PRINCIPLE #2
READ. WRITE. REPEAT

*"If you don't have the time to read,
you don't have the time or the tools to write."*

WHILE I THINK you'll quickly reach a point of diminishing returns when all you're doing is reading books on the writing process, I do think you should never stop reading fiction. Especially (but not exclusively) in your genre.

Many filmmakers have understood and used this idea to improve their film work.

As director/writer Amy Holden Jones recounted, "That's the thing that has helped me the most in my career.

"I remember when I first had to write a horror movie, when I first had to write a comedy, when I first had to write an action film, I would get myself down to the Writers Guild library or the Academy library, and I would sit down and read some of the best of the genre.

"No one would try to write a play who hadn't read plays. But all the time people try to write screenplays who don't sit down and read them. The vast majority of young writers you tell that to, the way they look at you, you know they're never going to do it."

Sadly, the same is often true of fiction writers: They'll dive headfirst into writing in a genre of which they really have only a minimal understanding.

Stephen King said it best when he wrote this in his terrific book on writing, called (cleverly enough), *On Writing*: "If you don't have the time to read, you don't have the time or the tools to write. If you want to be a writer, you must do two things above all others: read a lot and write a lot. There's no way around these two things that I'm aware of, no shortcut."

Before I started writing my *Eli Marks Mystery Series*, did I read every book in the cozy mystery genre?

I did not.

But I did read a ton of them.

Lawrence Block's *Burglar* and *Keller* series. Sue Grafton. Janet Evanovich. Agatha Christie. Lisa Lutz. And more. The good, the bad and the ugly.

And even though I'm now several books into not one but two mystery series, I continue to read genre fiction. Anthony Horowitz. Richard Osman. Louise Penny.

But at the same time, I also watched (and rewatched) movie mysteries. *Murder on the Orient Express* (the first one). *The Last of Sheila*. *Sleuth* (the first one). *Deathtrap*. Even episodes of *Columbo*.

Plus, long-form television productions, such as *Magpie Murders, Only Murders in the Building,* and Hugh Laurie's excellent version of *Why Didn't They Ask Evans?* (This last one employs one of my favorite but seldom-used tropes in well-written mysteries: a story where the answer to the crime is right there in the title. The same is true of *The Last of Sheila* and *You'll Like My Mother*).

Regardless of your genre, you should read (and continue to read) other authors, to help you gain a further understanding of the intricacies of your chosen form. And while you may glean some insight from the best in your category, there is also much to be learned from the examples where the writer may have fallen a bit short.

It's often easier to see what someone is doing wrong (and hopefully not repeat it in your work) than to completely understand what they're doing right.

BEYOND THE SCREEN QUESTIONS

- When was the last time you read a book from your genre?
- What related media are you watching that is in your genre?
- What did you learn from the last bad book you read?

Film Suggestions

Movies About Writers

Adaptation

The End of the Tour

Can You Ever Forgive Me

Barton Fink

PRINCIPLE #3
EXPLOIT THE UNIQUE

"If it ain't personal, it ain't no good."

THERE'S one idea that smart filmmakers have benefited from over the years: If you're lucky enough to have access to something that people don't see everyday, find a way to make it part of your movie.

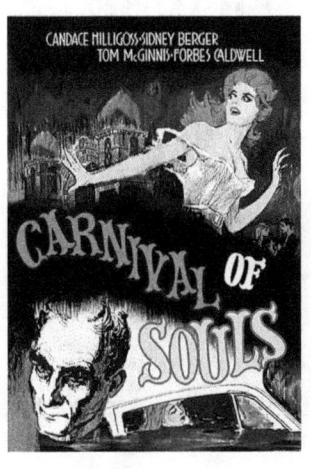

Director Herk Harvey recognized the value of that idea when he drove past an abandoned amusement park on his way home from a business trip. He realized the site would make a unique and compelling location for a movie. It was something most people had never seen before.

"It was sunset, and I was driving back to Kansas from California when I first saw Saltair," Harvey recalled. "It's an amusement park, located at the end of a half-mile causeway out into the Great Salt Lake. I felt I had been transported into a different time and dimension. I couldn't believe what I was seeing. I stopped the car and walked out to the pavilion. The hair stood up on the back of my neck. It was the spookiest location I had ever seen.

"When I got back to Kansas, I discussed Saltair with my friend, co-worker and writer John Clifford," Harvey continued. "We agreed that with the Saltair location, and others that we had locally, we just might be able to develop a script for a feature film."

The result? His classic film, *Carnival of Souls*.

For writer/director Tom DiCillo, it was one martini too many which inspired his most personal film.

"I was invited to the wedding of my wife's cousin," DiCillo explained. "I had a martini. I had never had a martini before in my life. And I said, 'Wow, if that's how you feel after one martini, let's have another one.'

"It was after the third martini that this guy came up to me. And he says, 'Oh, Tom, it's great to see you, man. You're so lucky, you made *Johnny Suede*, you made a movie. Lights, camera, action.'

"And I just erupted at him. I said, 'Shut the fuck up. Making a movie is one of the most tedious, frustrating, intense experiences I've ever had in my life. And not even just getting the money. What about when you're getting ready to do a shot and suddenly something screws up and the actor's moment that they've been working on for hours just disappears and you never get it back again?'

"Well, that's where I had the idea. I swear, right there at that moment, I thought, 'You know, that could make a film. Just confront a director with an endless number of disruptions and see what happens.' And that's where the idea was born."

That became his classic film, *Living in Oblivion*.

For filmmaker Roger Nygard, it wasn't his personal experience but that of a friend which became the basis for an early movie.

As Roger recounted to me: "My friend, Joe Yannetty, had written a one-man show about his experiences selling cars. I read portions of that and he told me some of the stories. And I said, 'You've got to make a movie about this. These stories are incredible.' So that's where it started.

"Joe and I worked together writing the script, based on his experiences, which is a process for me as a screenwriter that works best. I almost always work with a writing partner. My writing style is that I tend to write with people who have had interesting life experiences, but don't necessarily have the desire or the fortitude or the persistence to bring it to the screen."

They worked together on a script and the result was the now classic low-budget genre-buster, *Suckers*. (The genre-bending aspects of *Suckers* will be explored more in *Principle #4: Stay in Your Lane*.)

"Write what you know" could easily win the award as the Biggest Writing Cliché That Is Actually True. There is tremendous power in your own experiences and perspectives.

Roger Nygard said it best when he told me, "I never got a job as a CIA agent, never went into the Marines, never became a fireman or a cop, didn't go on the road and get arrested or sell cars. Your own life is often the first and best place to start for a screenwriter."

And that works for novel writers as well: the best and strongest angle you can offer is your own unique perspective, based on your life experiences. And—oddly enough—the more you stick to the reality and specifics of your situation, the more universal the story will become.

As director Tom DiCillo explained, "Whatever you write, you have to tap into something personal for yourself. I used to have an acting teacher who said to me, 'If it ain't personal, it ain't no good.'

"I absolutely believe that if you can find a way to tap into something that's very personal, and then make a creative leap from there, that's the best way to do it."

However, in order for this to work, you have to be willing to be honest and dig deep.

According to Roger Nygard, "You have to bare yourself to the world in order to write something that other people will be interested in reading. It's not easy. It's hard. You've got to write things that you wouldn't even tell your shrink. Those are the screenplays that really stand out."

Now this is not to say that every story you write should be a literal autobiography, because no one wants to see that. But you should draw on your own emotions and experiences to create real, truthful scenes.

Writer Horton Foote *(Tender Mercies, A Trip to Bountiful)* put it this way: "You create what you observe, what you see around you."

It's all about telling the truth, whether you're writing about your life growing up in a small town in the Midwest ... or saving the world from an alien attack.

As director Bob Clark (*A Christmas Story, Murder By Decree*) told me:

"Be truthful. You've got to find your reality, no matter how broad what you're doing is. If you're doing the Marx Brothers, it's wild, it's bizarre, but somewhere in there has to be some truth, no matter how outrageous or absurd or fantastical."

Or, from the world of the novelist, here's the great Jasper Fforde on the subject:

"Readers are interested in the way a writer sees things; the unique world-view that makes you the person you are, and makes your novel interesting. Ever met an odd person? Sure. Ever had a weird job? Of course. Ever been to a strange place? Definitely. Ever been frightened, sad, happy, or frustrated? You betcha. These are your nuts and bolts, the constructor set of your novel."

Take a chance. Tell the truth. Readers will respond.

BEYOND THE SCREEN QUESTIONS

- What unique aspect of your life could you use as the basis for your story?
- Who have you met who would be a great character and a wonderful starting point for a story?
- What's unique to your world: your skills, your career, your neighborhood, your history, your town?
- Which of these unique things could you be using as a starting point for your novel?

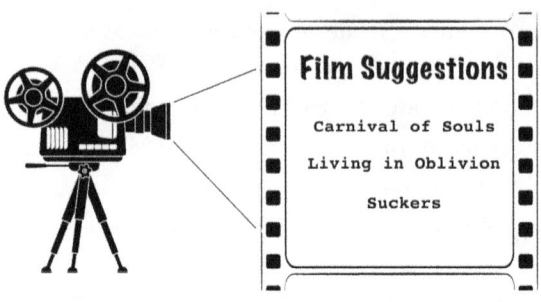

Film Suggestions

Carnival of Souls

Living in Oblivion

Suckers

PRINCIPLE #4
STAY IN YOUR LANE

"People just don't like genre shifts."

THIS IS a lesson novel writers and filmmakers must learn at their peril: Audiences are a fussy lot. While they may suspend their disbelief while watching or reading a story, that disbelief runs down a surprisingly narrow highway. Stray too far from that prescribed road and you'll lose your audience, perhaps for good.

If you've given them a cozy mystery, keep it cozy. Turning it into a blood-soaked thriller halfway through will only annoy your audience.

If it's a clean romance, don't turn it into spicy erotica in midstream.

If it's a spy thriller at the beginning, it better still be a spy thriller at the end.

That's a lesson director Roger Nygard learned the hard way. His film, *Suckers*, makes a serious tonal shift in its final third, changing from a workplace dramedy into a hard-hitting heist film.

Looking back on it, Nygard recognized the problem: "Audiences are not used to—and don't like it—when you shift from one genre to another. People just don't like genre shifts. They want to know what the genre is from the beginning, what's the level of reality of the story, and then you have to stick to it. If you don't stick to one genre, then you're either taking a chance or doing an art film."

That's not to say there's anything wrong with art films (or literary fiction in our world), if that's what you're setting out to write.

But a genre story is like a contract with the audience, with certain built-in guarantees. One of those guarantees is to play fair (i.e., if you set up rules that govern your universe, then you better stick to those rules). The other assurance is that you are going to take the audience where you promised, and then (with any luck), beyond that.

That doesn't mean you can't surprise them along the way—in fact, if you're not surprising them, you may want to start that re-write right now. But if you change horses in mid-story, don't get annoyed if the audience doesn't follow, but instead rewards you with one-star reviews and worse.

Robert Rodriguez and Quentin Tarantino learned this the hard way with their early film collaboration, *From Dusk Till Dawn*. Based on the marketing of the film, audiences came in expecting to see George Clooney in a heist-gone-wrong thriller. Imagine their surprise when the story suddenly shifted into a gory, vampires-on-the-loose tale.

George Romero ran into similar issues with his film *Martin*, in which the main character's possible vampirism is decidedly ambiguous.

"Initially I was thinking of doing it as a comedy," Romero explained. "I just got one of those ideas that comes to you in the shower: If there really were vampires, they'd have problems living hundreds of years. They'd have to keep changing their passport photos, they'd have all these practical problems. So, I wanted to do a comedy about the practical problems of a vampire in today's age."

(This was forty-plus years before *What We Do in the Shadows* came about. As always, Romero was well ahead of his time.)

"One day it just occurred to me that I could do this a lot straighter, and I could do a thing about somebody who's not a vampire at all," Romero continued. "I just thought that that would be more—not romantic—but it would be, in a way, more of a tender story. I wanted to just spin a vampire yarn a bit differently."

This unique approach—where the main character essentially thinks he's in a horror film and all the other characters think they're in a drama—made the movie a hard sell. It wasn't really a vampire movie, but that's how it was sold. And when horror audiences realized it wasn't a vampire movie, many of them stayed away.

You can benefit from that experience and those lessons learned by the other filmmakers mentioned: While audiences love twists and turns, in genre fiction you should stick to your own lane. And to do that, you need to commit to what you're writing. Which leads us nicely into the next Principle ....

BEYOND THE SCREEN QUESTIONS

- If you're writing genre fiction, can you define that genre?
- Are you mixing genres? Has this proven to be confusing for your readers?
- Are you staying in your lane?
- Does your story satisfy the key guarantees of your genre, while offering a couple surprises?
- What examples (in books and movies) can you think of where the story suddenly "changed lanes" halfway

through? How did you, as an audience member, feel about that unannounced genre shift?

Film Suggestions

From Dusk Till Dawn

Martin

Suckers

PRINCIPLE #5
YOU GOTTA BE COMMITTED

"The enemy of art is the absence of limitations."

THERE ARE many reasons why George Romero's first film, *Night of the Living Dead*, has entered the annals of film classics. But one key reason is this: Romero and his team set out to make the best darned zombie movie they could. (Although the term "zombie" didn't get applied to the film until well after it had achieved its well-deserved fame.)

They didn't apologize for it.

They weren't ashamed to be working in that genre.

They didn't wink at the camera, as if to say, "We all know that we're actually better than this."

"We were dealing with a fantasy premise," explained producer Russ Streiner. "In all aspects of the production, we treated it as a serious film. I think that overriding viewpoint is displayed in the final product. Once you buy the fact that the dead come back to life, it's treated in all other regards as a serious film."

Romero and his team were 100% committed to the movie they were making. That came through the lens. He saw the use of the genre as a way of telling a deeper story and he didn't feel the need to be ashamed of the genre, because it was central to the ideas he wanted to express.

"Really all my films are people stories," Romero told me. "Even at the heart of *Night of the Living Dead*, it's really about the people and how they screw themselves over and can't get it together. I like that theme tremendously: the lack of communication, the idea that people are still working their own fiddles and have their own agendas even faced with sea changes in the world."

Audiences responded to these ideas and have continued to be moved (and terrified) by the movie over fifty years later. It went on to become a classic in the genre, and is now part of the permanent film collection of New York's Museum of Modern Art.

That same obligation is required in whatever genre you've chosen: You have to be 100% committed to that form. If you're not, the audience can smell it.

If you think Urban/Vampire fiction is silly, your readers will sense that. So, while they may read your first book, they will avoid all subsequent volumes.

In the same way, if you think you're slumming when writing romance, your readers will agree and vote with their wallets.

Think space opera is silly? That will come through in your writing and the readers will tell you to blast off.

You need to be completely committed to the form, the tropes, the expectations and the requirements of your genre.

PRINCIPLE #5

Of course, that doesn't mean you can't flex your creative muscles within that framework. That's what Romero did with *Night of the Living Dead*, and all the subsequent genre films he made—sometimes successfully, sometimes not. *(See Principle #4: Stay in Your Lane.)*

Finding a creative spin within the tight boundaries of your genre is actually a requirement of the job. And in truth, it really will make your work easier.

Filmmaker Henry Jaglom had this quote from his pal Orson Welles tacked up above his editing console for years:

> *"The enemy of art is the absence of limitations."*

Filmmaker Jonathan Demme certainly understood this concept when he agreed to make *Caged Heat* for producer Roger Corman: Don't fight your limitations; make them work for you.

While his assignment was to make a standard Women-In-Prison picture, Demme was completely comfortable working within the confines of the genre because of the freedom Corman offered—that is, as long as he stayed within the bounds of the Corman Formula.

Demme explained it this way: "Having made sure that you accepted the rules of how to make a Corman movie, Roger then gave you an enormous amount of freedom to go ahead and do it. It wasn't until you started diverging from the formula, or from the approach, or—God forbid—went a moment over schedule, that you heard from him. And, of course, if you did stray from any of the pre-agreed conventions of making Corman movies, then you heard from him in no uncertain terms."

For his part, Corman was very happy with what Demme produced within the confines of the Corman Formula: "He made a really good picture that did what I asked him to do," Corman said. "It delivered the elements that the audience who wanted to see that kind of picture would come to see, yet at the same time there was an edge, a coldly humorous look at the film itself."

Corman went on to say that it was Demme's commitment to the genre that set him apart from other wannabe directors.

"The directors who say, 'Well, it's just a cheap picture, I'm going to knock this off,' are no longer in the business," Corman explained. "But the ones who said, 'Whatever the picture, I'm going to do the best job I can,' are the ones who stayed."

Corman agreed that it was that attitude that made him feel Jonathan Demme would have a successful career, even starting with a movie like *Caged Heat*.

"Jonathan told me, 'This is going to be the best women-in-prison movie ever made,'" Corman said, and then added with a wry laugh, "and it was at least close."

Being 100% committed to the book (and genre) you're writing in is no guarantee of its success. But a lack of commitment can easily be the first fatal step toward the book's subsequent failure.

BEYOND THE SCREEN QUESTIONS

- Are you proud of the genre you're writing in?
- Is that reflected in your writing?
- Can you think of examples (in books and movies) of creators who were clearly ashamed of the genre in which they were working?

PRINCIPLE #5

- Which genre limitations are you using to your creative advantage?

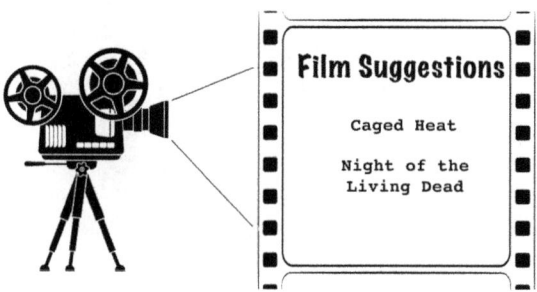

Film Suggestions

Caged Heat

Night of the Living Dead

PART TWO
PRODUCTION

Enough general theory. Now it's time to get down to some nuts & bolts ideas for taking your writing to the next level, with some ideas from our friends in the movie industry ...

PRINCIPLE #6
COME IN LATE, LEAVE EARLY

"I want people to get the feeling that they're being dropped right into the middle of a rapidly flowing stream."

AS I MENTIONED in the Introduction, the best screenplays are master classes in compression. A tremendous amount of storytelling needs to be accomplished in a short amount of time.

Every action, every line, every darned thing needs to add to the whole.

A podcast host once suggested to me that I must enjoy screenwriting more than writing books, as screenwriting allowed me to write "tons more dialog."

Nothing could be further from the truth. Most movies have a lot less dialog than most novels, simply because there isn't time for it.

A movie generally runs between 90 minutes to two hours. Look at the running time for the audiobooks made from most novels: they can easily run six to eight to ten hours. Granted, the majority of that running time might be the prose, but there's a whole lot more dialog in the average novel than in the average movie.

Consequently, in screenwriting (and in fiction) you should aim to get the most out of every line of dialog in every scene. Trim the fat at every opportunity.

And that principle begins with how you construct the scene in the first place.

Where you start it. And where you end it.

What's the trick?

Screenwriter William Goldman (*The Princess Bride, All The President's Men, Misery*) put it this way: "You always attack a movie scene as late as you possibly can. You always come into the scene at the last possible moment. Get on. The camera is relentless."

What's the best way to do that?

Try this: Think of each scene in your book like it's a party. Not a literal party, but a gathering of characters centered around one (or more) key plot points.

The best parties are the ones where you arrive after everything is up and running … and you leave before the party winds down.

And that works for the best scenes in movies: We jump in after everything is already in motion and we head off to the next scene before the current one runs out of steam.

We're taking things away and, in the process, making the scene stronger.

This is the idea behind the concept of Addition By Subtraction: by taking away one or more elements, you actually make the whole stronger.

(This idea will show up in later principles, as it applies in many ways to Principles #7 and #19 as well.)

It's remarkable how much you can often improve something by taking one or more things away.

PRINCIPLE #6

Once you realize this technique (thinking of the scene as a party), you will see it everywhere, in all kinds of movies and TV shows. All the fat has been eliminated.

Come in late. Leave early.

Director Michael Mann *(Manhunter, The Insider)* puts it this way: "I want people to get the feeling that they're being dropped right into the middle of a rapidly flowing stream. They didn't tiptoe in from the bank; they're just—boom!—in it. The stream's moving."

Not only is this a great way to add punch to your scenes, but in some instances, you can get an even bigger bang out of when you leave a scene and when you enter the subsequent scene.

A quick example:

In the original film of Mel Brooks' *The Producers* (1967), Zero Mostel and Gene Wilder track down the author of the worst play of all time, Franz Liebkind, on the roof of his New Yotk brownstone. He is tending to his pigeons.

They explain they want to buy the rights to his play (*Springtime For Hitler*) and Franz suggests they go inside to discuss it. *(If you want to watch the scene, it's about 31 minutes into the movie.)*

In the original script, this was followed by a long scene in his kitchen, where Franz demanded they raise a toast to Hitler, and then went on to say that he was one of The Fuhrer's favorites. He begins to recount all the good times they had together. The long speech continues with the two producers attempting to hum along to a song with Franz, who then suddenly comes out with this line: "Not many people know it, but The Fuhrer was a terrific dancer."

The editor of the film, Ralph Rosenblum, suggested to Mel Brooks that the humming, followed by this line, was the best entry point for the scene. The rest of the scene was not needed

This edit—from the three men on the roof to the three of them seated around the table—is not only funny on its own, but suggests everything that had come before in the kitchen without having to show it. We know they've been there a while. We know it's just gotten more and more awkward. The faces of Mostel and Wilder tells us all we need to know.

As Rosenblum explained, "The material shot in Liebkind's apartment worked magnificently on paper, but, for whatever reason, turned out flat on film. It killed Mel to lose a word. And here he lost over a hundred."

Rosenblum repeated that trick at the end of the scene, where Mostel hands a pen to Franz so he can sign the contract and says this will "make your dream a reality."

Rosenblum suggested cutting immediately after that line, even though the scene had continued through several more jokes. "That's where you want to cut, Mel. We'll drop the Siegfried oath, the Wagner music, the blood-ritual, and go straight to Mostel and Wilder on the sidewalk gloating over the contract."

Exiting the scene at that point made the entire transaction funnier and punchier and kept the movie moving along.

When you start looking for it, you'll see this technique—entering a scene as late as possible and leaving a scene as early as possible—working in all sorts of movies and TV shows.

It can also work in your storytelling and is best combined with a technique covered in the next section, called Cutting The Shoe Leather.

BEYOND THE SCREEN QUESTIONS

- Take a look at several scenes in your writing. What is the impact if you start later in the scene?
- How does it change things if you leave earlier?
- What can you subtract from your writing that will actually make the whole piece stronger?

Film Suggestions

The Producers
(1967 Version)

PRINCIPLE #7
CUTTING THE SHOE LEATHER

"Leave out the parts that readers tend to skip."

I MENTIONED EARLIER that I watched a lot of movie and television mysteries before I started writing my Eli Marks mystery series.

One favorite was *Columbo*.

Created by Richard Levinson and William Link (and brought to delightful life by Peter Falk), each episode employed a unique twist: Right up front we the audience saw who the killer was and how they committed the murder. The bulk of the story then consisted of watching Colombo as he put all the pieces together and finally cornered the killer.

While the stories were clever and Falk was brilliant, like many other TV shows from the era, *Columbo* employed a lot of what film editors have come to call "shoe leather."

Filmmaker and editor Roger Nygard defines shoe leather thusly: "The walk from here to there is not interesting. If somebody exits a scene and then enters another scene in a new location, we understand they had to walk or drive from one place to another. Keeping anything between the end of one scene and the start of the next will test the audience's patience."

In Columbo's world (and the rest of 1970s crime dramas), that meant a lot of walking to and from his car ... walking up to a suspect's house ... walking over to cops at a crime scene ... walking down a street to his next interview. Nothing related to the plot was delivered in these shots.

(I'm not including Columbo's fake exits, where he'd start to walk out of a scene and then at the last second turn and say, "Oh, just one more thing ..." Those moments were brilliant.)

And it's not just literal walking scenes. Shoe Leather is anything that delays you getting from Point A to Point B. It's filler and audiences will add in the details; they don't need to witness the journey.

Here's a classic example of eliminating shoe leather:

In the movie *Tootsie*, the first twenty minutes of the movie are spent learning about Michael Dorsey's (Dustin Hoffman) life as a struggling character actor. He accompanies his friend, Sandy (Teri Garr) to a soap opera audition, where she is trying out to play a hospital administrator. In the lobby, Michael learns that he has been passed over for an important Broadway audition. He races to his agent (director Sydney Pollack, in a terrific cameo) and learns that no one wants to work with him. Michael Dorsey is just too difficult.

He begs to be put up for any job, so he can raise the money to self-produce a play that he'll star in.

His agent tells him that's never going to happen. "No one will hire you."

Cut to Michael thinking as he says, "Oh yeah?"

This is clearly a moment of decision: He has decided to dress up as a woman to audition for the part on the soap opera to earn the money he needs to self-produce a play.

This is followed by what I think is one of the greatest edits in movie history.

A typical movie would have followed Michael's "Oh, yeah?" with a montage of him turning himself into Dorothy Michaels: Buying clothes, figuring out the make-up, choosing the wig, and on and on.

But that's not what *Tootsie* does. It cuts immediately from Michael's "Oh yeah?" to a crowded Manhattan sidewalk. People stream toward the camera. And after just a couple of seconds, we see Michael. But he is now fully costumed and coiffed as Dorothy Michaels.

Director Sydney Pollack explained his thinking behind this edit: "Originally, there were a series of long scenes of him learning how to be a woman: Talking to transvestites, talking to drag queens, learning how to fill balloons with bird seed, because they made the best breasts. Learning how to walk with a girdle on. I just took all of it out. It came out of my worrying about time pressure: we've got to get going, got to get going, got to get him work. Let's not take any of that time. Let's jump to it."

In short: They got rid of the shoe leather.

When you start looking for it, you'll see this technique employed in some of the smartest movies and television shows.

In some instances, the cut is nearly as classic as the movie itself: Like the cut from the bone tossed in the air ... to the space station in *2001: A Space Odyssey*. Or the cut from Peter O'Toole holding the lit match ... to the sun on the horizon in *Lawrence of Arabia*.

Sometimes an entire movie is about cutting the shoe leather. Martin Scorsese's *After Hours* is a master class of cutting out all the in-between parts and driving the story forward. (Kudos to editor Thelma Schoonmaker for her work on that and most other Scorsese films).

But most often, the removing of the shoe leather is something that—as a viewer—you don't recognize. That's because it wasn't needed in the first place and so its disappearance is never noticed. We move from Point A to Point B and the cut is so logical, and so in keeping with the story's momentum, that it feels not just correct, but inevitable.

But when the shoe leather has been left in—in a movie or TV show—as a viewer, you can really feel it. The story is sluggish. It drags. You feel like yelling at the screen, "Get on with it!"

The same can be true when reading a story that's been overloaded with shoe leather. There are long passages describing how the character got from Point A to Point B.

Or long, involved explanations based on the hours of research that you feel *have to be* part of the book.

Or flashback details that really don't add anything to the story, the theme or the character.

Writer Elmore Leonard was talking about eliminating shoe leather when he was asked for the best tip he had for writers.

He said this: "Leave out the parts that readers tend to skip."

He meant you should cut the shoe leather.

BEYOND THE SCREEN QUESTIONS

- Can you think of moments in your novel that are really just shoe leather?

- Why are those moments there? Are they helping or hurting?
- Think of two side-by-side scenes in your story. How could the storytelling be improved by cutting out all the in-between stuff?
- When editing your work, are there parts you skim past? Is it likely your readers will do the same?

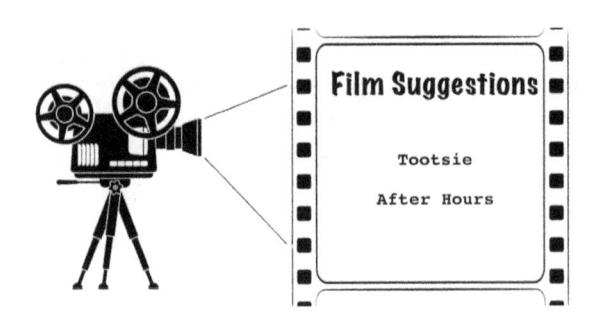

Film Suggestions

Tootsie

After Hours

PRINCIPLE #8
INTENTIONS & OBSTACLES

*"If a character wants a cookie,
he shouldn't just be able to get his cookie out of the jar."*

IF YOU DON'T HAVE conflict, you don't have drama. That's a basic tenet. And it's hard to argue with that.

Every scene needs conflict to drive it forward.

I didn't really understand what dramatic conflict meant until I started to watch *The West Wing* and followed up by reading interviews with its creator, Aaron Sorkin.

For Sorkin, it isn't about simply conflict. It's much more personal and it involves every character in every scene.

It's about intentions ... and obstacles.

This is how Sorkin explains it: "I kind of worship at the altar of intention and obstacle. Somebody wants something. Something's standing in their way of getting it. They want the money, they want the girl, they want to get to Philadelphia — doesn't matter. And if they can *need* it, that's even better. Whatever the obstacle is, you can't overcome it like *that* or the audience is going to say, 'Why don't they just take the other car?' or 'Why don't you just shoot him?' The obstacle has to be difficult to overcome. And that's the clothesline that you hang everything on — the tactics by which your characters try to achieve their goal. That's the story that you end up telling."

Although this is a great global approach to your story, it can also be used to turbo-charge every single scene—and do it without adding some outside element to create drama.

Director John Badham (*Wargames, Saturday Night Fever*) agrees: "If you can't break a dramatic scene down into actable objectives that can be described by strong actable verbs, the scene is no good. It has no place in the movie or the play. You may shoot it anyway, but it will always stop the movie cold. It contributes little or nothing to the overall story."

Writer Scott Frank (*Out of Sight, The Queen's Gambit*) explains it this way: "A movie script has to have conflict. Not just the overall plot, but even within a scene.

"Let me give you a dumb example: If a character wants a cookie, he shouldn't just be able to get his cookie out of the jar. The jar should be hard or impossible to get at. He has to climb on a ladder and the ladder breaks, and he's in a hurry. Every scene has to have inherent conflict. Nothing happens easy. As a writer you always want to be thinking, 'How can I turn this scene? What's in the way? What's the conflict here?'"

If you take this approach to every scene in your story (What does each character want? What is stopping them from getting it?), you'll find natural (not manufactured) conflict which feels real and makes your story more believable.

And the only way to achieve that is to give every character in every scene an intention and an obstacle.

While most of the scenes in my Eli Marks series are about Eli trying to find answers (it is a mystery, after all), within each scene I try to give him a unique intention and obstacle.

It can be as simple as trying to get out of a too-comfy couch or as inane as worrying about how to sneak a piece of hard candy from the bowl on his ex-wife's desk. But he always wants something and there is always something getting in his way.

Writer/Director Miranda July worked in a similar fashion when crafting the script for her film, *Me and You and Everyone We Know*. Although she substitutes the word "problems" for "obstacles." But it comes down to the same thing:

"Characters have intentions, whether you're conscious of it or not," she told me. "And pretty quickly there's a set of problems. So then much of the scene comes out of trying to solve problems. There's a certain point where there's just enough stuff where you establish problems and at that point you start solving problems."

Having trouble starting a scene ... or writing a scene ... or fixing a scene?

Ask yourself what's the intention for each character. And what's the obstacle in their way.

Not sure of an intention for a character? The world is full of options, but I often fall back on Elaine May's super suggestion:

"When in doubt, seduce."

BEYOND THE SCREEN QUESTIONS

- Take a scene you've written and write out the intention and the obstacle for each character in that scene.
- How does the drama of the scene improve when you sharpen each characters' intention or become more specific about the obstacle?

Film Suggestions

The West Wing
Seasons 1–4
Any Episode

PRINCIPLE #9
DON'T SPILL ALL YOUR POPCORN IN THE LOBBY (GIVE YOUR CHARACTERS A SECRET)

"Any good movie is filled with secrets."

IN THE LOW-BUDGET FILM, *The Anniversary Party* (written and directed by Alan Cumming and Jennifer Jason Leigh), at one point in the evening-long party, guests get up and offer speeches and gifts to the couple celebrating their anniversary (played by Cumming and Leigh).

The scene was unscripted. As Cumming explained to me: "For that scene, we asked the actors to make up their own speeches or to make their own things. We guided them about what perhaps their character might say, what their character's angle might be, but we left it up to them to make up their thing. It was really fascinating. We shot their stuff and our reactions at the same time. We were hearing it for the first time, which was really exciting."

That's the type of surprise you want to create for your readers as they're reading your story. You've guided them toward those moments, but you haven't spilled all the details up front. You've doled out information slowly, instead of providing an info dump in the first few pages. And then you surprise them at different points in the story.

In the classic film, *Butch Cassidy and The Sundance Kid*, the audience (and Butch) don't know the Sundance Kid has a secret. And we don't find out what it is until the fateful moment when the two of them are perched on a cliff, with the Super-Posse fast approaching behind them.

It's only at that point, when pressed against the wall, that The Sundance Kid admits his long-held secret. It's the reason he's resisting making the leap into the river far below.

"I can't swim!"

This is a secret that adds drama and suspense (and humor), while also providing more depth for the character.

(It's also a secret which clearly amuses Butch, who famously replies, "Why, are you crazy? The fall will probably kill ya!")

Don't confuse this with a major plot point secret: Keyser Söze's real identity in *The Usual Suspects*, the reveal of Norman's mother in *Psycho*, or the identity of the murderer in any mystery.

Instead, these are character moments which you hold back, to provide gas to your story's engine. Or moments that provide depth and background for one of your characters.

For example, in the classic film *Harold and Maude*, there is a brief moment where Harold realizes that in the past Maude had spent time in a World War Two concentration camp. At about sixty-nine minutes into the movie, the two are holding hands. Harold glances down and there's a super brief insert shot (about two seconds long) where we can see the remnants of a number tattooed on Maude's wrist. No further mention is ever made of this quick shot, but it's impact on the film and on our understanding of Maude's character is immediate and lasting.

As director Mike Nichols observed: "Any good movie is filled with secrets."

Other examples of well-placed secrets include *(skip this part if you're a freak about spoilers for shows and movies that have been around forever)*:

- President Bartlett's secret that he has MS on *The West Wing*.
- Don Draper's secret that he really isn't Don Draper, but is in fact Dick Whitman, on *Mad Men*.
- The Mandarin is actually an actor in *Iron Man 3*.
- The real reason the castaways are stuck on *Gilligan's Island* (Gilligan didn't tie the anchor down before throwing it overboard.)

The secret doesn't have to be earth-shattering, but it needs to be at least interesting. And perhaps surprising. And we shouldn't learn it right away: Audiences like it when you don't tell them everything about a character all at once, but dish it out slowly.

And, sometimes, characters will tell you their secrets before you reveal them to your readers. Here's another story from Aaron Sorkin about *The West Wing*:

"We were a few days into shooting the pilot when I noticed that Richard Schiff was wearing a wedding ring. I went to him and said, 'You know, Richard, I didn't think Toby was married.' He said, 'Yeah, I don't think he is either.' I said, 'Why is he wearing a wedding ring?' and Richard said 'I was leaving that to you to figure out.' And so it came to be that Toby was still in love with his ex-wife."

Think about all the surprising things you've learned about friends you've known for years. It happens more often than you might realize.

- After knowing my wife-to-be for a while, I was surprised to learn she had once been questioned by the KGB while on a school trip to Russia.

- A co-worker at a small company, who was the furthest thing from Fred Astaire, surprised everyone when he and his wife hit the dance floor at a Christmas party; they were a phenomenal dance duo.
- A vendor casually mentions he owns two homes: One for his family and another for his massive G.I. Joe collection.

Finding out something new about someone you thought you knew well can add a lot of kick to your story. The secrets are out there and can be used to your advantage, story-wise.

BEYOND THE SCREEN QUESTIONS

- Are you slowly revealing your main character, or overwhelming your readers with tons of information jammed into Chapter One?
- Do your characters have any secrets you haven't revealed yet? If so, when would be the most (or least) opportune time to do that?
- What secret could you give your characters that might provide some surprising depth?

Film Suggestions

Butch Cassidy & The Sundance Kid

The West Wing
"17 People"
(Season 2, Episode 18)

PRINCIPLE #10
SAVE THE CAT, KILL THE CAT. I DON'T CARE. JUST CREATE AN EMOTIONAL CONNECTION

"It all goes to emotion."

HOW MUCH DO you care about Hannibal Lecter? Do you feel you had an emotional connection to the sociopathic, murderous cannibal?

No?

Consider this: At the end of *Silence of the Lambs,* Lecter is clearly on his way to murder his nemesis, Dr. Chilton. ("I'm having an old friend for dinner.") He's not just walking; he's happily sauntering toward this homicidal encounter.

Quick: At that moment, who were you rooting for?

I'm willing to bet your money was on Dr. Lecter. Like it or not, the movie created an emotional connection between you and everyone's favorite cannibal. You wanted him to win. Once it was clear he was never going to hurt Clarice, you didn't care one way or another what fate befell the snotty Dr. Chilton.

Which is a primary goal in all storytelling—movies, plays, books: Make a connection.

You and Hannibal at the end of *Silence of the Lambs*?
Emotionally connected.
Mission accomplished.

Creating an emotional connection between your main character(s) and your audience is the secret to making a hit movie … and writing a successful book. While story, pacing, surprises are all important, it's the connection you create between your reader and your characters which is going to make the biggest difference.

Writer/director Jon Favreau explained it to me this way: "It all goes to emotion. If you're emotionally engaged, everything is going to be funnier, more satisfying, scarier, everything. It's that emotional connection that you feel."

Favreau believes this emotional connection was one of the reasons *Swingers* was so successful with audiences.

"It's the one thing that you really have going for you in a small movie," he explained. "You're doing something that's so real and usually so personal that you have a level of emotional engagement that you will not get in a high-budget, high-concept movie."

Okay. So, how do you create that connection?

A common trope among screenwriters is the idea of *Save the Cat*. Based on the book of the same name by Blake Snyder, the concept is often reduced to the simple notion that your hero should do something heroic or endearing early on (such as save a cat), so that the audience sympathizes with the character, thus becoming emotionally invested in the story.

There's actually a lot more to the Save The Cat concept, which is a 15-point formula for structuring a successful screenplay, with an emphasis on storytelling, creating compelling characters, developing a strong theme and a unique plot. But people often reduce the whole thing to just making sure your character does something nice or selfless early in the story.

But it doesn't have to be that. Cats need not be involved.

In fact, your character doesn't have to do much of anything to deserve the desired emotional connection. Instead, if someone else is horrible to your main character, you can build sympathy for a character, even if they are somewhat reprehensible (i.e., the Dr. Lecter example above).

A less murderous illustration can be found in the Marx Brothers movie, *A Night at the Opera*. Early on there's a scene with Harpo's boss, Lassparri, literally beating Harpo to punish him for … well, for being Harpo. Later in the film, you feel no sympathy toward Lassparri as the Marx Brothers exact their vengeance against him, piling indignity after painful indignity upon the hapless villain.

As comedian and director David Steinberg pointed out: "Harpo, in the first scene of *A Night at the Opera*, is being beaten by Lassparri. When you see a guy physically abusing someone else, you can take all your time and slowly torture this person comedically. And the audience's sympathies will never leave you."

Creating this relationship between your readers and your characters is a primary goal in pulling readers into your story. Accomplish this connection and you're well on your way to a successful and compelling story.

BEYOND THE SCREEN QUESTIONS

- What steps have you taken to help your readers connect with your main character?
- What's your version of Save the Cat in your story and with your main character?

- Do you have an unlikeable main character? If so, what can be happening in the world around this character to make readers root for them?

Film Suggestions

A Night at the Opera

Silence of the Lambs

PRINCIPLE #11
CALLBACKS—DON'T FORGET TO REAP WHAT YOU SOW

"Audiences love a callback."

NOTHING DELIGHTS an audience more than a well-placed callback: A reference to an earlier moment in the story which takes on a different and deeper meaning when you remind the audience about it later in the story.

The greatest callback of all time may be from *Casablanca*. In that 1942 classic, a phrase uttered early in the story in reference to dealing with possible insurgents ("Round up the usual suspects") makes a second, more meaningful appearance at the story's climax.

Rick has shot Major Strasser, a Nazi commander who was about to make a phone call to prevent the plane to Lisbon from taking off. On that plane? Resistance hero Victor Lazlo and his wife (and Rick's former lover), Ilsa Lund. This has all been witnessed by the morally-dubious Louis Renault, the Chief of Police. As policemen arrive to determine what has happened, Louis quickly explains the situation to his men: "Major Strasser has been shot!"

A quick look between Rick and Louis. Are they truly friends? Or is everything in Louis' life transactional? A suspenseful pause. And then Louis continues.

"Round up the usual suspects."

The police run off to do that, as Rick and Louis head off into the night (with the classic closing line: "Louis, I think this is the beginning of a beautiful friendship").

"Round up the usual suspects" is the perfect callback; a seemingly innocuous moment from early in the story which returns later in a surprising manner. But, in this instance, it wasn't planned. This classic callback was discovered not only after the script had been written, but while the film was in production.

The two screenwriters who worked on the script during the shooting of the movie, brothers Julius and Philip Epstein, wrote scenes while filming continued, creating a three-page outline of how all the story elements would come together in the final, pivotal airport scene. But the one element which eluded them was how Rick could shoot Strasser and get away with it. The answer came—as some of the best ideas often do—as a bolt out of the blue.

"Julius Epstein has always said that the ending was solved when he and his brother—while driving to the studio one day—turned to each other and said in unison, 'Round up the usual suspects,'" explained Aljean Harmetz, author of the definitive book on the movie, *Round Up the Usual Suspects: The Making of 'Casablanca.'* "Rick would kill Strasser, and [Louis] Renault would protect him."

Callback deployed. Problem solved.

"Round up the usual suspects" is a perfect example of taking something from earlier in your story and re-purposing it for greater depth later on.

The trick for writers is recognizing when you've placed the seeds for a strong callback and then waiting for the right moment to harvest them.

For the Epstein brothers, the key was recognizing (and remembering) the phrase and then understanding the impact it could have at the end of the story.

Callbacks can take all kinds of different forms.

- In the *Veep* pilot, Selina expressed the hope that a big news story—something like Tom Hanks dying— would occur and distract the media from her current scandal. Then, in the final episode of the series, Selina's funeral is pre-empted by a big news story: The death of Tom Hanks.
- In the comedy film, *Stuber*, the silent nature of the hero's electric car is mocked early in the story. Then, in the climax of the movie, the very fact of the car's silent running helps to save the day.
- In the classic horror film, *Henry: Portrait of a Serial Killer*, a simple prop which appears early in the film (a guitar case) takes on terrifying implications later in the story.
- In the indie-comedy, *Go*, the nearly unnoticed disappearance of a minor character halfway through the movie comes back as a surprise at the end. This is also known as the Something We Forgot trope, which can be found in many stories and movies, including *Airplane!* and *Home Alone*, (which is essentially a feature-length version of the Something We Forgot trope).

PRINCIPLE #11

There may be no greater use of callbacks than in the movie *Back to the Future*. The entire script (by Bob Zemeckis and Bob Gale) is really just one long, continuous callback.

I won't begin to list all the callbacks, as such a compendium would require a book all its own. Suffice it to say that Zemeckis and Gale did a brilliant job of creating a web of connected threads through the film (and to a lesser extent, throughout the trilogy) that bounce and ping off each other in many delightful ways.

This talent for callbacks was also evident in their earlier film, *Used Cars*, where tossed off references (the impending arrival of driving school students, the irrational fear of red cars) return with surprising implications later in the story.

Whether you're building your story around the callback(s), like Zemeckis and Gale did so brilliantly ... or combing through your first draft to find gems to help you cross the finish line in your final draft, like the Epstein brothers ... callbacks can be a secret weapon which you can deploy to surprising effect during your story.

A word of warning: Don't harvest your callbacks prematurely. Years ago, I was reading a cozy mystery *(Principle #2: Read. Write. Repeat)*. In the course of the story, a secondary character purchased a weapon (a taser). Then, within a chapter or two, that taser came in *very, very handy* during a fight scene. Suspiciously handy.

This was not a good callback for two key reasons: First, too much was made of its (highly questionable) purchase. And second, the need for the taser occurred too closely to its appearance in the story.

A good callback should seem innocuous when it first appears ... and it should have disappeared from the reader's mind long before it makes its surprising and impactful return.

But that warning doesn't mean you should shy away from building callbacks into your story. Properly employed, they can be one of your strongest writing tools.

As Daniel Scheinert, the co-writer/co-director of *Everything Everywhere All At Once*, explained: "Audiences love a callback. It's such an easy storytelling maneuver: 'Oh, it came back!' Part of why they like (callbacks) is it tells them someone confident and in control is telling this story. It's like (you're telling the audience), 'Don't worry, I've got you. I've got a plan.'"

BEYOND THE SCREEN QUESTIONS

- Are you currently employing any callbacks in your story?
- Are your callbacks well placed, innocuous, and far enough from their use in the latter portion of the story?
- Have you combed through your draft, looking for callback seeds you may have planted without realizing it?

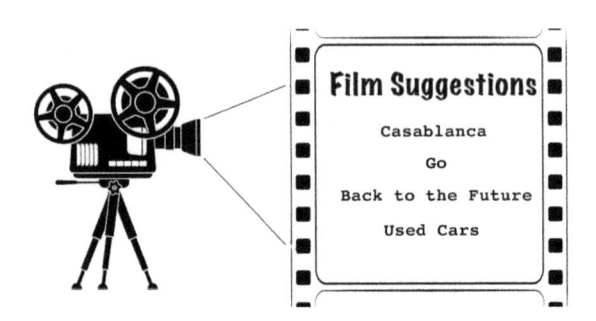

Film Suggestions

Casablanca

Go

Back to the Future

Used Cars

PRINCIPLE #12
GREAT EXPOSITION DOESN'T SOUND LIKE EXPOSITION

"To write exposition brilliantly is hard."

EXPOSITION (THE INTRODUCTION of key story elements) is a requirement of fiction writing. The audience needs to know who's who, what they're doing, where they are, and their relationships with other characters.

In short, they need to know what's going on.

The trick in good writing is to make the delivery of that information painless and invisible.

This is something really good movies seem to do effortlessly.

On the other hand, some movies and TV shows find ways to achieve this a little less elegantly than others.

We've all seen police procedurals where our hero shows up at a crime scene and is "brought up to date" by a co-worker who seems to have absorbed all the pertinent details in record time. Even though this secondary character may have arrived on the scene only moments before, they already possess a compendium of facts about the crime. It's a clunky way to do it, but it gets the job done.

A similar trope, particularly during police interrogation scenes, is to come into the scene late *(see Principle #6)* and then have one of the characters recap what they've discussed up to that point. ("Okay, Dave, tell me again what happened when you stepped into Sean's apartment ...?")

But there are more elegant ways to deliver exposition.

This can often be accomplished by mixing the needed exposition with something more fun or interesting. As Mary Poppins so wisely explained, just a spoonful of sugar can help the expositional medicine go down.

A retro example: in the old *Mission: Impossible* TV series, the plot for each episode would be cleanly laid out for Mr. Phelps (and the audience) via a tape-recorded message from an unseen boss. During this expositional passage, Phelps would sort through photos of all the characters (which were often the actors' actual headshots, which was a smart, cost-saving idea), as we learned the details of the story and the characters. And then the tape would disappear in a fizzy puff of smoke. Mission Impossible? Hardly. In terms of delivering needed exposition, it was Mission Accomplished.

Citizen Kane kicks off with a nine-minute newsreel, recounting the life (and death) of its main character, Charles Foster Kane. Subtly satirizing the newsreel format (which was popular at the time of the film's release), this movie-within-a-movie nicely sets up the key incidents and people of Kane's life, which we'll discover in greater detail as the film goes on.

This technique (using another media to inform characters within the media we're watching) was new at the time, but has now become a standard cliché. It's morphed into a quick news report seen on a nearby television, delivering key information just at the moment it's needed in the story.

This cliché was nicely parodied in Tom Stoppard's 1968 play, *The Real Inspector Hound*, in which a character turns on a radio just in time to hear: "We interrupt our programme for a special police message. The search still goes on for the escaped madman who is on the run in Essex. County police led by Inspector Hound have received a report that the man has been seen in the desolate marshes around Muldoon Manor."

The play also parodies the convention of characters giving out more information than one normally would do in that situation. Moments later, the character who had turned on the radio answers the phone with the following: "Hello, the drawing-room of Lady Muldoon's country residence one morning in early spring. Lady Muldoon and her houseguests are here, cut off from the world, including Magnus, the wheelchair-ridden half-brother of her lady-ship's husband Lord Albert Muldoon, who ten years ago went out for a walk on the cliffs and was never seen again."

A simple and often dramatic solution for exposition is to bury the necessary information within the dialog of an argument.

Michael Dorsey's (Dustin Hoffman) argument with his agent (Sydney Pollack) at about the twenty-minute mark of *Tootsie* is a great example of delivering key exposition within a barb-filled debate between the two characters. We learn about Michael's reputation for being a brilliant but difficult actor, his frustration at not being able to get work, his need for $8,000 to produce his friend's play, his unwillingness to compromise, and his extremely slim prospects at achieving his goal.

And all of this is nicely disguised as a rapid-fire (and often heated and funny) exchange.

Another approach is to use a new character as an excuse for bringing the audience up-to-speed.

Writer/director John Sayles used this technique to introduce his large (and largely unknown) cast in his low-budget classic, *The Return of the Secaucus 7*.

As Sayles explained: "When you have a lot of characters in a movie, and none of them are stars, none of them are very well-known character actors, you're probably going to have to introduce them a couple times, and have those introductions be something about who they are and who they are going to be in the script, so the audience doesn't feel lost."

In order to accomplish that introduction, Sayles included a key scene early in the film where one character identifies each of the others, while also spelling out their relationships to the rest of the group. Although that may seem heavy-handed, Sayles did it in the guise of having a new character—someone unfamiliar with the group—enter the movie and need to be brought up to speed. In that context, the scene is fast, funny—and very helpful for an audience trying to get their bearings.

The Big Chill, a movie often compared to Sayles' lower-budget film, accomplishes the same task in a different manner, by introducing us to the main characters with a montage during the film's opening title sequence. This allows us to see each of them in their own environment for a few moments, before bringing them all together for their college friend's funeral. This technique doesn't give us a lot of information but does offer a quick sketch to introduce the film's key players.

Highly technical information can sometimes bog down a story: even though an audience needs to understand the mechanics of a situation, the delivery of those key elements can ruin your pacing.

Two top-grossing films solved this problem in elegant and similar ways.

In *Titanic,* one of Bill Paxton's crew members uses an animation and his own dramatic descriptions to demonstrate to Titanic-survivor Gloria Stuart the steps the great ship went through after hitting the iceberg. *(This is at around the 18 minute mark in the movie.)*

Since she was actually *on* the ship when it went down, Gloria Stuart hardly needed what she refers to as "this fine forensic analysis." However, it's extremely helpful for the audience, as it provides us with the key steps (in chronological order) of the disaster. Because of this early explanation, later in the film we always know what's going on when the ship begins to sink for real.

Jurassic Park also had some dense technical information to deliver to its audience. In particular, it was to explain how the DNA of dinosaurs (found in mosquitoes trapped in amber) had been harvested to create the new crop of dinosaurs which inhabit the about-to-be-opened park. Using the premise of an interactive theme park ride, the characters in the movie (and the audience watching), learn all that information from an animated character called Mr. DNA. *(This is at about the 27-minute mark in the movie.)*

CJ's press briefings on just about any episode of *The West Wing* were often great ways to deliver technical information (along with wisecracks). The same was true of her prep scenes before the briefings, which were effective at bringing us up-to-speed on key plot points and technicalities.

Planning scenes before a big battle fulfill the same function: They tell us key information about what's about to happen, so we can react when things do or don't go our way.

The film *Gambit* has probably the bizarrest approach to exposition: The first third of the movie is spent telling us all the steps of an upcoming, high-stakes robbery. The rest of the story uses that information to comic advantage, as the audience watches things go wrong at every step of the plan which had been detailed to us earlier.

In movies, actors often carry the brunt of the exposition. Cary Grant reportedly said something along the lines of "stars don't do exposition," and was (they say) always trying to hand off exposition lines to the other actors.

Actor Richard Jenkins (*The Shape of Water, Cabin in the Woods, Six Feet Under*) appears to agree, saying "Exposition—every movie has it. But if you're talking to your brother and you say, 'You're my brother. And do you remember when our mom died last year? And she was sick, you know, with cancer. And do you remember our uncle came over and he shot Jimmy in the arm that day?'

"It's like, does your brother have Alzheimer's? I mean, what —why are we having this conversation? It's for the audience. You want to stay away from that stuff. But to write exposition brilliantly is hard. There are things the audience has to know about you. But how did they find that out? And that's when you see the skill of the writer."

Excellent exposition can take many varied forms: A bizarre form of communication, a parody of a traditional form, a new character, an argument, a recap for someone just entering a scene, a fun presentation, a planning session …

These are all (relatively) painless ways to bring the audience up-to-speed, which in its purest form is the raison d'être for exposition.

BEYOND THE SCREEN QUESTIONS

- Look at where you're providing exposition in your work. Are you giving this information to the reader in an artful way?
- Are you providing too much information all at once?
- How could you be sprinkling exposition throughout your story? *(Think back on Principle #9: Don't Spill All Your Popcorn in the Lobby)*

- Finally, ask yourself this: Does my reader <u>really</u> need all the information I'm providing? Am I giving it to them because I simply <u>have it</u>, or because they <u>need it</u>?

Film Suggestions

Tootsie

The Return of the Secaucus 7

Titanic

Jurassic Park

Gambit

PRINCIPLE #13
THEATER OF THE MINIMAL

"See the world in a grain of sand."

HAVE you ever heard of this movie? A small group of people venture into the woods searching for evidence of a supernatural entity, bringing along video cameras to document their experience. Something bad happens. Most of them end up dead. And all that remains is their video footage, which may or may not reveal what happened to them.

No, sorry. It's not *The Blair Witch Project*.

It's *The Last Broadcast*.

Produced a year before *Blair Witch* rocked the indie world, *The Last Broadcast* set some records of its own, including being the first feature to skip the traditional transfer to film and hit theaters digitally.

But another key thing the movie did was to convince me of an important principle: the secret to persuading the audience you've captured reality is found by judiciously offering them just a few key details.

As William Blake so sagely put it, you can help them "see the world in a grain of sand."

In other words, if you're writing a Dan Brown-style adventure yarn, you don't need to give the audience page after page of facts and figures about the elements of the hunt. Just a few well-placed tidbits are often enough to keep readers turning pages.

"We called it Theater of the Minimal," *The Last Broadcast's* co-director Stefan Avalos explained of his film. "It's amazing how little it takes to convince people. You only need small clues to make something seem convincing. And I found it amazing how readily people believed the movie, based on just a couple little pseudo-realities within the movie."

Many of those convincing details were found in the numerous newspaper articles and legal documents which appear on-screen in the movie. Fun fact: None of those props ever existed as hardcopies, but were instead created electronically, using Photoshop and other off-the-shelf graphics programs.

Director Joan Micklin Silver understood the value of the Theater of the Minimal approach as well, for purely economic reasons.

However, the few period details her small budget allowed her to offer probably made her film, *Hester Street*, stronger in the long run. Although she longed for the deep pockets of larger films, those spectacular moments were simply not possible with the money she had available to produce her low-budget movie.

This was particularly true when it came to shooting a key

scene, showing her main character's arrival at Ellis Island.

She explained the budgetary problem to me this way: "In *Godfather II*, there's a very long scene in Ellis Island in which there's an overhead traveling shot. The boy who will grow up to be Robert DeNiro is sitting on a bench and you see him in isolation, all by himself. It's just a stunning shot. When it came time to do Ellis Island [on *Hester Street*], I had to do what I think just about all low-budget filmmakers do: you make a part work for the whole.

"You have to ask yourself, 'What's the most important thing about this?' And I decided that it was the separation between the ones who were already there and the ones who had just arrived. Therefore, I thought if I could do some sort of a fence or something that would keep the two groups apart, that would help to say what I wanted to say. I remember that the fence cost about $800, which was a huge portion of our budget. I think it worked."

As a novelist, of course, you face no such budgetary concerns. You can take your readers anywhere and can tell them everything.

But don't.

Don't tell them everything.

Please don't tell them everything.

Just give them the right details and let them fill in the rest themselves.

When I come across novels where the writer has decided to provide every detail about every room, every character, every sunset, and a myriad of other unnecessary details, I am reminded of what Jeff Goldblum's character warned in the first *Jurassic Park* movie: "Your scientists were so preoccupied with whether or not they could, that they didn't stop to think if they should."

The truth is, the best stories rely on small but telling details which bring their world to life without overwhelming the reader.

BEYOND THE SCREEN QUESTIONS

- Look at any chapter from your novel. Are you providing more detail than necessary? *(Remember Principle #9: Don't Spill All Your Popcorn in the Lobby)*
- What are the key details your reader really needs to know?
- Are you providing details simply because you have them and "don't want to waste them"? Or are they truly necessary to the telling of your story?
- How can you make the part work for the whole?

Film Suggestions

The Last Broadcast

Hester Street

PRINCIPLE #14
KEEP LESTER AWAKE

"If it's not moving the plot forward, it doesn't belong in the script."

WHO IS Lester and why do we care if he's awake or asleep?

Director Stuart Gordon (*Re-Animator*) learned about Lester while he was directing plays in Chicago before moving to Los Angeles. Lester was the husband of one of the theatre's patrons.

As Gordon explained to me: "Lester was notorious for falling asleep in the middle of the plays, and sometimes snoring. So, I was always, in the back of my mind, thinking 'We've got to keep Lester awake. We have to have something going on every moment to keep Lester from falling asleep.' And I think I'm still trying to keep Lester awake."

As authors, we too need to keep Lester in mind while crafting our stories. Are we keeping it interesting? Is the story surprising? Are we always moving forward?

Are we, as Elmore Leonard suggested, leaving out the parts that readers tend to skip? *(See Principle #7: Cutting the Shoe Leather)*

I think this was expressed in its best and simplest form by

director Brian Levant (*Beethoven, The Flintstones, Jingle All The Way*): "My first goal is not to bore anybody."

Dan Futterman, the Oscar-nominated screenwriter of *Capote*, learned this from his wife, who is also a writer. He shared drafts of the script with her during his writing process. "She was clear and strict with me, saying 'If there are any scenes where people are just talking, cut it, because if it's not moving the plot forward it doesn't belong in the script.' And that was important to learn. It has got to move."

Not only should every scene move your story forward; each scene should also contain its own intrinsic tension.

As Stuart Gordon explained: "Every single scene should have some tension in it. You really can't have any scenes with people just sort of sitting around and relaxed. You have to find the tension in each scene. What you really want to do is to keep people on the edge of their seats all the way through."

(*Look back at Principle #8 about giving each character in a scene their own intention and obstacle.*)

While there is the old cliché of people reading a book at night to help put themselves to sleep, your goal should be just the opposite: You want to keep them awake, turning page after page, unable to nod off because they are so engaged in the story.

The lesson here is to look at every scene with a cold, clear eye and ask yourself: "Is this moving the story along? Or is it just going to put Lester to sleep?"

If it's the latter, then it's got to go.

BEYOND THE SCREEN QUESTIONS

- Be honest: When reviewing your manuscript, are there sections (paragraphs) that you tend to skip over?
- If so, go back and look at them more closely. Are they adding tension? Humor? Moving the story forward?
- Or are they likely to put Lester to sleep?

- Do the endings of each of your chapters make the reader want to turn the page and find out what happens next? Or turn off the light and go to sleep?

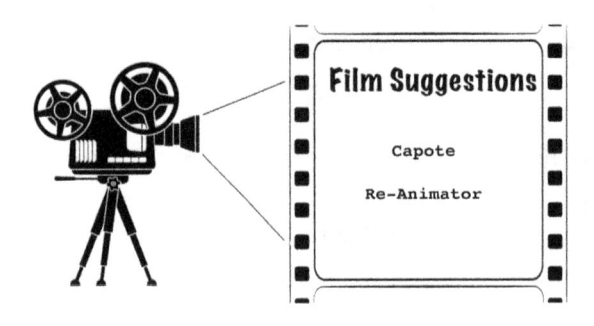

Film Suggestions

Capote

Re-Animator

PRINCIPLE #15
ALL'S WELL THAT ENDS WELL

"We've been conditioned from childhood to expect good to triumph over evil. When someone subverts that a bit, people can get rubbed the wrong way."

I DON'T THINK anyone would dispute the importance of a strong (and satisfying) ending. It's the last thing the audience (and the readers) will experience, and it can either leave them elated ... or deflated.

The world of the movies can be broken into many categories, but there is clearly one sub-section of shame: movies whose endings were not merely disliked, but consistently derided.

Planet of the Apes (the Tim Burton version). *Indiana Jones & The Kingdom of the Crystal Skull*. *Now You See Me*. Even M. Night Shyamalan has two entries on many people's lists of bad endings: *The Village* and *Signs*.

The world of fiction has its own hall of shame when it comes to disappointing endings: *Gone Girl*. *Mockingjay*. *My Sister's Keeper*. Even J.K. Rowling was added to many people's list, with *Harry Potter and the Deathly Hallows*.

Let me repeat a couple of those names: Tim Burton. M. Night Shyamalan. J.K. Rowling. Proof that anyone—*anyone*—can stumble when it comes to crafting the right ending for their work.

The trick is balancing the ending you want ... with the ending your audience needs. What follows are a few cautionary tales.

Sometimes it's our favorite moments in what we write (or shoot) that are doing us the most harm.

For filmmaker Kevin Smith, it was his original ending for *Clerks*: The convenience store clerk, Dante, says goodnight to the video store clerk, Randall, and prepares to close the store. One final (unseen) customer enters. Dante tells him that they're closed. Suddenly the customer shoots Dante and robs the store, leaving our main character dead on the floor.

Brian O'Halloran, who played Dante, remembered his initial reaction to the idea: "I thought the script was funny, but I hated that ending. I never thought it worked. I just thought it was too quick of a twist. I remember going to Kevin, and I believe I told him I didn't like the ending. But we did it anyway."

Smith, however, loved the surprise conclusion he had devised: "To me it was like, that's the ultimate joke. He is not even supposed to be there, and he gets killed."

Cooler heads prevailed.

"Right before we went to Sundance," Smith recalled, "[Film agent] John [Pierson] said, 'There is one thing you have to do with the movie: you have to cut that ending off.' And I knew that a few people who loved the movie, hated the ending. But John was like, 'I really think you should cut the ending and if I am wrong, you can put it back later. You can talk to the distributor and ask if you can put it back.' So, we cut it right before we went to Sundance."

That was a smart choice.

Cutting that downer ending made for a stronger experience for audiences ... and opened the door for two subsequent sequels as well. *(See Principle #19: Kill Your Darlings.)*

For the ending of *The Last Broadcast*, co-directors Stefan Avalos and Lance Weiler opted to take a big creative risk, which may or may not have paid off, depending on who you ask.

Audiences are split on the ending; the people who love it really love it, and the people who hate it loathe it. (One website review of the movie opened with this heading: *"The Last Broadcast. Worst ending ever? Maybe."*)

Without giving away any twists, I can say that the ending turns what appears to be an objective documentary into a subjective narrative, with a twist that is surprising and original (although not strictly logical).

For their part, the filmmakers couldn't be more delighted with the controversy.

"The ending was one of the first things we thought of for the movie," Avalos said. "Instead of breaking down the fourth wall, we were putting the fourth wall up. We were really excited by that idea."

For Weiler, the ending is the perfect encapsulation of the theme of the movie.

"The movie really takes you on this ride. The point we were trying to make with the film was that you can't necessarily believe everything that you see. And when we twisted it at the end, we really wanted it to feel like a punch, to leave you breathless.

"That was a very bold choice on our part, to all of a sudden break that wall and go into what was, effectively, a narrative. I think people have trouble with endings sometimes when they don't get what they feel is a final resolution or a final answer. I think people like things wrapped up, in nice, cohesive packages."

On the flip side of that sentiment is Neil LaBute's controversial first film. (As opposed, I suppose, to all of his subsequent controversial films.)

That film, *In the Company of Men,* is a 1997 black comedy-drama. It tells the story of two white-collar businessmen, Chad and Howard, who hatch a cruel plan to emotionally terrorize and manipulate a vulnerable, deaf woman they both meet. The film follows their journey as they carry out their plan, and the effects it has on all three of their lives.

Some audiences have come away from the movie appalled, more than anything else, by the fact that (spoiler alert!) Chad gets away scot-free and doesn't pay for his horrible behavior.

However, for LaBute, that was the whole point:

"I felt that it was truer to the

story that Chad goes unpunished. A lot of people are more keen to give what the audience wants, which isn't always the truth, it's perhaps more what they've come to expect.

"We've been conditioned from childhood to expect good to triumph over evil. When someone subverts that a bit, people can get rubbed the wrong way. But all the Chads in this world don't get caught. To spend ninety minutes being creative, and then five dashing it all by making the audience feel good about themselves isn't worth it to me."

Your ending is the last thing your readers are going to experience. If your ending hasn't brought your audience to the satisfying conclusion of an emotionally-fulfilling journey, their opinion of everything that has come before it—as wonderful as it might have been—can be seriously jeopardized.

(Just ask the folks who watched the last episodes of *Lost* and *Game of Thrones*.)

So, proceed with caution ... and, just to be safe, test your ending on your beta readers. Which leads us very nicely into Principle #16: Previews!

BEYOND THE SCREEN QUESTIONS

- What movie and book endings disappointed you? What did the creators do wrong?

- What endings stand out for you as perfect examples of a strong ending?
- Is your current ending inevitable, surprising and satisfying?
- Be honest: If you were a reader of your book, what would your response be to your ending?

Film Suggestions

Clerks

The Last Broadcast

In the Company of Men

PART THREE
POST-PRODUCTION

The end is in sight, but there is still much to be done and many changes to be made before your finished product is actually finished.

PRINCIPLE #16
PREVIEWS!

"But it's always good to get some feedback, because you're kind of in a vacuum."

FILMMAKERS HAVE RECOGNIZED this fact since the first silent movies hit the nickelodeons: There's real value in putting your unfinished work in front of a real audience before you really finish it. Really.

In some cases, studios insist upon it. In others, the filmmaker is genuinely interested in hearing (or feeling) audience feedback. And the only way to get that is to put your work in front of an audience.

Some movies changed drastically after their previews: Glenn Close's demise in *Fatal Attraction* was completely re-written and re-shot. Molly Ringwald ended up with Andrew McCarthy instead of Jon Cryer in *Pretty in Pink*. Even the ending for *Clerks* was radically altered before it went to Sundance. *(See Principle #15: All's Well That Ends Well.)*

For other movies (and moviemakers), the preview is a chance

to see if the audience "gets" their movie. Christopher Guest and Michael McKean recalled an early preview for *This is Spinal Tap*.

Guest: "Michael and I (stepped out) to get some popcorn, and there were two young women who came out in the middle of the movie, and one of them said to the other one, 'These guys are so stupid!'"

McKean: "Well, they were right."

Guest: "And one of the cards said, 'What did you like about it?' And the person who wrote it said, 'It's in color.'"

Novelists can emulate this preview process by employing what's referred to as beta readers. These are folks (friends, previous readers, writing group compatriots) who read through the book before its publication. It's a chance for the author to get some feedback on what's working (and what isn't).

We'll get into how to process that information in the next chapter *(Principle #17: Getting Notes)*.

But before we do that, let's turn to our cinematic brethren to see what value they've gleaned (or not) from putting their nearly finished movies in front of an unsuspecting audience.

For the makers of *The Last Broadcast*, previewing their film was an opportunity to evaluate how well their story was working.

Co-director Lance Weiler explained it to me this way: "I think when you know a story really well in your own head, there are certain little connecting things that maybe other people don't pick up on. The test screenings we did made us a little more aware of certain things that we took for granted. It was pretty much where we wanted to go, it just needed some tweaking. But it's always good to get some feedback, because you're kind of in a vacuum."

Putting your book in front of beta readers offers that same

feedback opportunity, letting you know if you've taken certain plot points for granted or perhaps left your readers a little adrift at other points.

For makers of comedy movies, putting a version in front of a test audience is ideal, because you can finally see where the laughs are (or aren't).

"For a comedy person, it's a must," explained director Betty Thomas *(Dr. Dolittle, The Brady Bunch Movie)*. "My movies have all changed for the better because of tests. I just like to feel when an audience is with it or not. I've taken to videotaping the screenings so that when a studio executive later tells me a particular joke didn't work, I can prove that it did."

Director Ron Howard agreed. "You can't really know what your film is saying until you put it up in front of an audience. Playwrights have their period of previews, they have that opportunity, so why shouldn't filmmakers?"

Producer Roger Corman concurred, telling me: "I'm a firm believer in putting the film, at least one time, before an audience. You always learn something. In about half the pictures we've made, they play well in the sneak preview, and we send them straight out. In the other half, we will make some edits, some changes, according to the audience reaction in a sneak preview."

Ron Howard thinks this is particularly true of comedies. "Funny is funny. There is nothing like showing a comedy to audiences to really understand it. Roger (Corman) was very dogged to making sure we paid attention to what we learned in those preview screenings."

Of course, novelists hardly ever get to hear the laughs their stories produce, but early readers can alert you as to whether or not they found it funny … along with pointing out other problems or areas of confusion.

The outside prospective provided by preview audiences can help filmmakers shape (and re-shape) their stories. And that process can work for you as well, as your beta readers report back to you with their feelings.

Here are a couple extreme examples:

During the editing of *The Blair Witch Project*, the filmmakers decided to make a substantial change to their feature film. They came to the conclusion the story would be stronger if they eliminated the majority of their documentary interviews, which had been the bulk of the film. They instead opted to tell the story via the footage their actors had captured in the woods. The original plan had been that this footage would play a much smaller role in the finished movie. *(See Principle #19: Kill Your Darlings.)*

It was a radical move and it wasn't until they put the film in front of preview audiences that they realized the new approach was working.

Co-director Daniel Myrick explained it to me this way: "We screened a very long cut of the student's footage. It was set up like a very traditional test screening, where we called in all of our friends and their friends and whoever would give up a couple hours of their afternoon and come check out this film. We handed out questionnaires, about what they liked and didn't like. And from those questionnaires you can draw a consensus about what people are turned on and turned off by.

"And we had more than a few comments telling us, 'You know, this really is your movie. We don't really want to break away from the narrative story of what's going on here.' That test screening was really helpful in that respect."

Marvelously zany humor.

For the classic film, *Monty Python & The Holy Grail*, the test screenings went from really bad ... to bad ... to better ... to perfect. But it was a long, painful process.

"The first showing of *Holy Grail* was a total disaster," remembered co-director Terry Jones. "It was a disaster, an absolute disaster. People laughed for the first few minutes, then just silence all the way through the rest."

"It was one of those evenings when Python flopped," actor/co-writer Michael Palin explained. "There was some laughter and there was some enjoyment and there was polite applause at the end, which felt like a spear in the guts, because it was clear that the audience had been, by and large, disappointed."

The problem, they determined, was that in their quest for medieval realism, they may have gone too far.

Executive Producer John Goldstone explained it this way: "What had happened was, [co-directors] Terry Gilliam and Terry Jones decided to make it as real as possible, to have a soundtrack that was very real, bone-crunching and everything. It was all as authentic as they could possibly get. Neil Innes did the music, it was a sort of semi-religious chant that in fact was kind of too real. And so it wasn't getting the response from the audience that we'd expected."

The troupe re-grouped quickly after the early screenings, to discuss what worked, what didn't, and what was needed to make the movie as funny as they knew it could be. And they did it again after the next screening. And the screening after that.

"There were thirteen screenings of *Holy Grail*," recalled actor/co-writer Eric Idle. "We dragged it towards being funny."

Thirteen previews turned out to be the film's lucky number,

because from that point on the movie worked and became the classic we know today.

With any luck, your book won't require a major tossing out of three-quarters of your material (as *The Blair Witch Project* did) ... or multiple trips back to your beta readers (such as *Monty Python & The Holy Grail* required).

But the beta reading process can help you put your book into its final shape, point out confusing plot points, and provide clarity. Plus, fresh sets of eyes always seem to find those few pesky typos which you somehow missed.

Of course, all the news may not be positive. Taking notes is an art all in itself. We'll cover the best way to do that next.

BEYOND THE SCREEN QUESTIONS

- Have you assembled your small team of beta readers for your book?
- How willing are you to make changes based on what you're hearing?

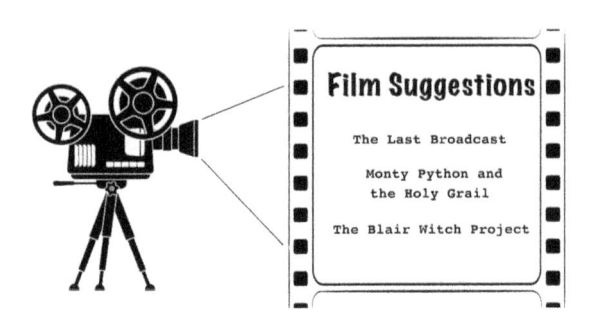

Film Suggestions

The Last Broadcast

Monty Python and the Holy Grail

The Blair Witch Project

PRINCIPLE #17
GETTING NOTES

"That's the main thing, to really know what you have to fix."

JUST AS THERE'S an art to screenwriting, so too is there an art to receiving and reacting to notes.

Most screenwriters agree that having a handful of close associates look over your script is a good thing. They also agreed that you don't need to react to every single note you get.

As director/writer Amy Holden Jones put it, "Usually if I show a script to five people, I will pay a lot of attention to repeating comments. So, if three or four of the five people say, 'The end doesn't work for me,' then I know the end doesn't work. If one of the five says 'It doesn't work for me,' and four of the five say it's fine, then it's less of an issue."

Writer/director Dylan Kidd (*Roger Dodger*) agreed, telling me, "I do have people that I turn to and that I care about what they think. But my feeling is that unless the comments match something I already felt in my gut anyway, or if every person has the same comment, then I know I have an issue. I generally have found that putting too much stock in feedback can get confusing, because people are going to have a hundred different opinions."

Writer/director Whit Stillman (*Metropolitan*) takes a different tack, suggesting that the writer is better off, ultimately, by going it alone. "I'm not sure it's very helpful having a lot of voices in on the creation of a script. I think they try to smooth things and homogenize things and explain things. It's better making it a kind of goofy voyage and ride, when you have to just be honest with yourself about what you're doing and where your mistakes are and what isn't working."

Of course, identifying the problem is not to be confused with finding the solution. And, as might be expected, everyone has an opinion.

Writer/director Miranda July (*Me and You and Everyone We Know*) came to that realization after her screenplay went through the Sundance Labs, where some advisors provided extremely specific thoughts on what they felt needed to be changed in her script.

Miranda recalled, "Some were like, 'Here's what you've got to do. In the second act, she's going to run away.' They'd give you these really specific notes, and you're like, 'Oh my god, this is a nightmare.'

"But you learn a really great process for getting notes from producers: you learn how to distill what the problem is from the solution they're providing."

Also, readers will often find fault with one area of the story, not realizing the blame for that problem lies elsewhere in the script.

As writer/director Kenneth Lonergan (*You Can Count on Me*) explained, "It doesn't mean that the real problem is where it appears, because it can be like a medical symptom: the symptom may not appear where the cause is.

"You can acknowledge that there's a symptom somewhere that someone points out—maybe—but you certainly should be very skeptical when they start talking about what the solution is or what the nature of the problem is."

Miranda July agreed: "Everyone's solutions are their solutions. So I came up with other ones. That's the main thing, to really know what you have to fix."

That's a sentiment worth repeating: The main thing is for you to figure out what needs to be fixed. And then come up with your own solution to the problem.

Getting (and giving) notes is a real art form. While there are no set rules, Ken Weber in his terrific book, *Maximum Entertainment 2.0*, does a stellar job of laying out some helpful ground rules for the process. I'll refer you to his book for the full story, but will highlight a couple key ideas here:

GETTING NOTES

- Unless this is part of a writer's group process, try to receive notes in private. Not at a dinner or a cocktail party.
- If the notes are coming at you verbally, write them down. You might think you'll remember everything later, but odds are you won't.
- Don't argue. Don't explain. Just take notes *(see above)*.
- Before doing anything with the notes, wait a day. Or a week. Let them settle.
- Be sure to thank your note giver.

At some point, you may be asked to give notes to another writer. Here are a couple pointers for when you find yourself in that situation:

GIVING NOTES

- Ask before offering to give notes. Not all notes are wanted.
- As with getting notes, do it in private.
- Lead with the positive notes.
- Try to be as specific as you can, without overwhelming the author.
- And, if possible, provide your notes in writing.

Again, I refer you to Ken Weber's excellent *Maximum Entertainment 2.0*, which is required reading for anyone who wants to step up on a stage for any reason.

But there's also lots of good stuff in the book (like how to give and receive notes) for non-performers as well.

Finally, remember that when someone gives you notes, it's just one person's opinion. And people can be wrong about these sorts of things.

For example, United Artists, Universal and (ironically) Disney, all passed on a little movie called *Star Wars*.

I'm just saying.

BEYOND THE SCREEN QUESTIONS

- How have you reacted to notes in the past?
- Do you take notes personally, or are you able to look at the process objectively?
- Have you given notes to other writers?
- How does that affect the way you receive notes?

Film Suggestions

You Can Count on Me

Me and You and Everyone We Know

Metropolitan

PRINCIPLE #18
THERE IS NO SHAME IN RESHOOTING

"Art is never finished, only abandoned."

THE ABOVE QUOTE has been variously attributed to the likes of W.H. Auden, Jean Cocteau, Paul Valéry, and Leonardo Da Vinci.

Regardless of who first said it, the sentiment is timeless.

You are nearing the end of what, on occasion, may have felt like an endless process: the final steps before you call your book "done."

Your beta readers have reported back.

You've made note of their notes.

And there were <u>lots</u> of notes. Certainly, more than you expected.

Suddenly you feel like you're back to square one. There is so much to do. So much to fix. So much so much so much.

Not to worry. You're not the first person to visit Re-Write Island and you won't be the last.

Filmmakers hit this bump in the road all the time.

They get deep into editing and realize they need to go back

and shoot a little more (or a lot more), in order to make their movie work.

The same way you need to go back and do a little re-writing. Or a lot of re-writing.

So, take a deep breath and relax. It's all part of the process.

When Doug Liman directed *Swingers*, he built re-shooting right into his production schedule.

"Part of my strategy for shooting this film," Liman said, "was that I left two days at the end of the schedule to re-shoot anything that didn't come out, so I could take these wild chances. We ended up scheduling 18 of the days, and the other two days were sacred."

Liman required every second of those extra two days, because there were chances he took that hadn't paid off. But there were also lots of chances which had, and he feels that without that two-day safety net, he might not have taken those risks.

"The movie wouldn't be the movie that it became if I hadn't done that," he said.

The lesson we can take away from this? Don't freak out if some of your writing chances didn't work in this draft. Just build the re-write into your schedule.

Other filmmakers didn't employ that type of forethought, but had to reshoot for other reasons, some practical, some artistic.

For director Jim McBride, his work on his classic faux documentary, *David Holzman's Diary*, wound up being what amounted to a complete, page one re-write.

Here's how he recounted the story to me: "I was working at a company that sold land in Florida, and they did it through films. I was serving an apprenticeship there, learning to shoot, learning to edit, stuff like that. I got this idea for what was later to become *David Holzman's Diary*, and they let me borrow their equipment on weekends.

"We shot a bunch of stuff, almost all of it improvised—and not very well, I should add—and then as we were shooting, I got fired. So, I packed it all up into a box and put it in the trunk of my car. And I went around looking for a cutting room that someone would lend me so I could put these pieces together. And when I finally did locate a cutting room a couple of weeks later, I went to the car and opened it up and discovered that someone had stolen the film.

"In those days, 16mm was associated with porn, so my guess is that's why somebody took it. They must have been terribly disappointed. And I was terribly disappointed myself, but as time went by, I was kind of relieved because it really sucked. But somehow the experience of doing it made me realize how I should have done it differently."

With that hard-earned knowledge, eight months later the cameras rolled again on the second (and final) version of *David Holzman's Diary*.

For first-time filmmaker John Cassavetes, the making of *Shadows* was a long and arduous process. The film mixed scripted scenes with improvised moments and was both a labor of love and a trial by fire.

After finishing the movie and screening it for audiences, Cassavetes did one of the hardest things for a filmmaker to do: he took a cold, hard look at the film and realized he had missed the mark.

"I could see the flaws in *Shadows* myself: it was a totally intellectual film, and therefore less than human. I had fallen in love with the camera, with technique, with beautiful shots, with experimentation for its own sake. All I did was exploit film technique, shooting rhythms, using large lenses, shooting through trees and windows. It was filled with what you might call 'cinematic virtuosity' for its own sake, with angles and fancy cutting and a lot of jazz going on in the background."

However, the film was not a total loss; he felt there were salvageable elements.

"The one thing that came to me after I had laid it aside a few weeks was that now and again the actors had survived all my tricks. My producers, Maurice McEndree and Seymour Cassel, got together and said, 'Now look, John, we're going to have to do some reshooting. We have all the faith in the world in you, but you're an amateur.' So, I decided to reshoot it."

Yes, that's right. Reshoot the movie. That was a bold move, and a move that proved to be successful.

"We started again, and I tried to shoot it from an actor's standpoint," Cassavetes recalled. "And I think we succeeded because the actors are wonderful, whereas before you couldn't see them for all the trees and cars."

Cassavetes ended up reshooting about three quarters of the movie in two weeks. And he was glad he did, feeling that the new version was much closer to his original vision.

"The second version is completely different from the first version. In my opinion, it is a film far superior to the first. The cinematic style which was so prominent in the first gives way to the emotional experiences that the characters encounter. The emotional expressiveness of the first version dissipated in its generality—the emotions were not precise and particularized. The second version was more exact."

Sometimes we can't see what our work is supposed to be until we get a good look at what it isn't supposed to be. That can be a hard thing to face. But if you're honest with yourself (and with your work), you can tackle the task of re-writing, re-energized by what the first pass taught you.

Writer/director Alex Cox put it this way: "Write until it's finished. Then re-write it. There were fourteen drafts of *Repo Man*."

Your re-writes may amount to a simple clean-up ... or a total overhaul. But it's a great opportunity to step back and see if you're achieving what you set out to accomplish. And if you've missed the mark, it's your chance to take another shot at the target.

But it's also a time to face one of the biggest challenges writers (and filmmakers and all artists) occasionally have to confront head-on.

We'll tackle that next.

BEYOND THE SCREEN QUESTIONS

- Have you built re-writing into your production schedule?
- Are you excited by the re-writing process? Or dreading it?

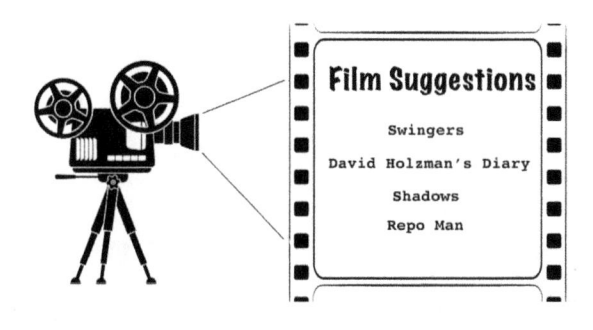

Film Suggestions

Swingers
David Holzman's Diary
Shadows
Repo Man

PRINCIPLE #19
KILL YOUR DARLINGS

"It's hard to throw stuff away."

THE TITLE of this chapter has often been attributed to William Faulkner, although a similar thought ("Murder your darlings") was expressed earlier by Arthur Quiller-Couch.

However, I prefer the version popularized by Stephen King: "Kill your darlings, kill your darlings, even when it breaks your egocentric little scribbler's heart, kill your darlings."

As you may have realized from the three previous chapters, once you've written something in your book, there is no guarantee that it will make it to the final draft. Or that it should. We often find (to our deep and regrettable sorrow) that it's our favorite parts which need to get the axe.

Playwright and screenwriter Eric Bogosian put it this way: "Editing and deleting is as important as writing and sometimes just as difficult because it's hard to throw stuff away."

As previously mentioned, the makers of *The Blair Witch Project* jettisoned a huge chunk of what they had assumed would be their movie. It became clear to them the footage in the woods was stronger and better than the footage they'd intended for the main body of their movie. *(See Principle #16: Previews!)*

"We initially shot two phases of *Blair Witch*," co-director Daniel Myrick told me. "One was kind of a framing device, which was more like a traditional documentary, where you had interviews."

The other phase was all the "lost" footage of the filmmakers in the woods.

"Initially when we went out to shoot, we were only hoping to get fifteen or twenty minutes of the students' footage in the woods," Myrick continued. "We never anticipated that we'd have enough to cut an entire feature. It was always our goal to get just a handful of really good moments within the construct of the storyline, and then much like *The Legend of Boggy Creek* or an *In Search of...*, have it sprinkled throughout what would be more of a traditional documentary.

"And when we came back with so much great footage, and because we had scripted our time out in the woods with a complete narrative arc, we came back to the edit and said to ourselves, 'You know, we have a movie in just this footage. It's a very risky movie, but we do have a movie.'"

"We knew it was different, and a risk," agreed co-director Eduardo Sanchez. "But as rough and as raw as it was, we knew we should leave it alone."

"It was a very tough decision for us to jettison that original concept for the film," Myrick admitted. "I was more resistant to jettisoning that stuff. But once we did, I was really glad that we decided to do that, because ultimately, that became the movie."

Making that sort of major decision is hard. Particularly if you've been working on the project for years ... and years.

David Lynch spent four years meticulously crafting his first feature, *Eraserhead*. But it wasn't until he saw the movie for the first time with an audience that he realized he had a handful of darlings who needed to be executed.

"The pacing is slow in *Eraserhead*, and that's great," Lynch said. "I love the feel of it. But I think some scenes were dragging it down to where the pacing was painful. It was pushing you out of the film. It was just too long. So that night [after the premiere], I made a decision. In my heart, I knew that some of these scenes had to go. I'd never been able to quite do it, but when you feel an audience not reacting, then you can do it. So out they came.

"After that screening, I drove over to [Director of Photography] Fred Elmes' house. I sat in the car with Fred, and I told him every scene I was going to cut, and exactly where it was gonna be cut, so I wouldn't forget it. And the next day, I cut the composite print, which you're not supposed to do. But I just cut it and rearranged it, because I'd been wanting—needing—to do it. It was so long this other way, it was not working.

"It's still long for a lot of people."

The issue of 'it's too long' is one shared by many people about *2001: A Space Odyssey*. Yet after that film's premiere, director Stanley Kubrick famously cut (and destroyed) about 20 minutes from the film.

As Kubrick explained: "I always try to look at a completed

film as if I had never seen it before. I usually have several weeks to run the film, alone and with audiences. Only in this way can you judge length. I've always done precisely that with my previous films.

"For example, after a screening of *Dr. Strangelove* I cut out a final scene in which the Russians and Americans in the War Room engage in a free-for-all fight with custard pies. I decided it was farce and not consistent with the satiric tone of the rest of the film. So, there was nothing unusual about the cutting I did on *2001*, except for the eleventh-hour way in which I had to do it."

This is a nice reminder that even the big names have trouble killing their darlings, but ultimately, they do what needs to be done.

Not all excisions are as large-scale as on *Blair Witch*, *Eraserhead* or *2001*. But each one is a big deal for the filmmaker who has to sacrifice a much-loved scene.

For Alan Cumming and Jennifer Jason Leigh, the darling they needed to murder was the final scene in their movie, *The Anniversary Party*.

"I think the best decision we made was cutting the last scene," co-director Cumming explained. "It was a scene where it was the next morning and she's in the hot tub and I come and join her. We give each other our anniversary presents, and we have a big scene talking about the fact that our marriage has broken up."

Cutting such a major scene is never an easy decision. But in order to tell the best story you can, you sometimes have to think about how it can be improved by taking things away rather than adding them.

(It's the Addition by Subtraction idea, first mentioned back in *Principle #6: Come in Late, Leave Early.*)

"We weren't particularly happy with the last scene, we were having trouble editing it," Cumming said. "And then we thought, if we just cut that scene, the movie will end and we can take a shot from the beginning—the very first shot—and put that at the end and bookend the whole thing.

"I think you're always feeling that you have to be absolutely scrupulous about explaining everything and bringing everything to a conclusion," he continued. "And it was quite liberating to remove the scene. It's really interesting, you just don't need to necessarily force-feed the audience every detail. What it did was leave the audience having to think more about what happened in the movie, instead of being told that it was over now and this is the end."

In the filmmakers' minds, that ambiguity actually made the film stronger and more interesting.

"We don't know what will happen to them," co-director Leigh explained. "We examine a lot of relationships in the movie and they're all kind of beautiful and funny and flawed, and yet they somehow sustain. And maybe they'll make it. Maybe not, but maybe they will."

One of the best-known examples of the "Kill Your Darlings" dictum was the planned ending of *The Big Chill*. As it was originally scripted (by Lawrence Kasdan and Barbara Benedek), the movie was set to end with a major flashback. In it, we'd see all the characters from the movie as they appeared in their twenties.

And we'd finally meet the unseen, missing character, Alex, whose suicide kicks off the movie.

The character of Alex was played by a then mostly-unknown Kevin Costner.

Editor Carol Littleton explained her feelings about that scene to me:

"After I first read the script, we sat down and I said, 'I feel very uneasy about this flashback. I just don't think you need it.' And Larry [Kasdan] with his nasal, West Virginia voice, said, 'Carol, I can't believe you said that. You are so wrong. I can't believe it. You are so wrong.' So, I dropped it. When somebody says you're wrong, you drop it.

"Then when we were shooting it, I said, 'This looks like a masquerade, with everybody in long hair and beads.' And Larry said, 'Carol, you are so wrong. The reason I wanted to write this script was because of this idea.' And I said, 'Yes, Larry, you're absolutely right. It's a wonderful idea. You may have needed that scene to write the script, but you don't need the scene for the movie. At all.'"

Littleton makes an important point there and it's worth repeating: You may have needed that scene to help you write the story, but it is no longer necessary to tell the story.

However, Littleton's dealings with that pesky flashback were far from over.

"In the editing, we put that flashback everywhere," she explained. "We took it out of the ending, we put it up front, we put it in the middle, we put it in pieces, we spent a lot of time trying to get the flashback to work.

"We showed it to the studio with the flashback and the suits came in and the guy who was in charge said, 'This is not funny. Take it back, re-do it. Start over again.' And then he said, 'While you're at it, that flashback is a stinko scene.'

"So, we showed it to them the next time with an audience and the movie still did not work as well as it should. So, I said, 'Larry, why don't we devise an ending, drop the flashback, have two screenings—one with the flashback and one without—and let the audience tell us which one is more effective?'

"Well, at the screenings, it was clear that the version without the flashback was better. And the next day, when Larry came into the cutting room, he said, 'God dammit, Carol, I wanted you to take that thing out from the beginning! How many times do I have to tell you I'm right?' That's how funny he is. He's wonderful."

Here's writer/director Nicholas Meyer (*Time After Time, Star Trek: Wrath of Kahn, The 7% Solution*), with his point of view on killing your darlings:

"You are very likely to vest what you've written with greater importance than it deserves. 'Oh, Christ, don't cut that line. That's the heart of the movie.' Maybe it is and maybe it isn't. [In many instances], the one thing that no longer seems to belong is the seminal, catalytic scene that inspired the whole work.

"A certain kind of amateur refuses to pull that scene out, out of some slightly misguided sense of, I don't know what, an abstract concept that was inspirational but now doesn't fit. You outgrew it. You fight and argue. But there's only one rule in show business. If it works, leave it in."

And if it doesn't work, it has to go.

It may have been the scene that inspired you to write your novel. It might even be your favorite scene. You think it's the best thing you've ever written.

But if it doesn't belong in the story, it has to go.

It's doing you more harm than good.

Coming to that realization—and then making that painful edit—is a difficult but necessary part of being a real writer.

It's no picnic, but it has to be done.

I'll end this section by returning to a sentiment from *The Big*

Chill. A minor character (Karen's husband, Richard, who leaves after the first night), says something that has stuck with me and that applies in many situations, including the need to kill your darlings:

"The thing is, nobody said it was going to be fun. At least, nobody said it to me."

BEYOND THE SCREEN QUESTIONS

- Can you identify any "darlings" in your story? (Segments you love but which don't really need to be part of your novel.)
- Did your beta readers share any reactions to that scene?
- Take a cold hard look: Does it change things for the better (or worse) if you lose your darling?
- If the 'darling' in question is a large piece of writing, have you considered releasing it separately, perhaps as a free reader magnet?

Film Suggestions

The Blair Witch Project
The Anniversary Party
Eraserhead
The Big Chill

PRINCIPLE #20
DON'T HESITATE TO HESITATE

*"It's never done. Writing is re-writing.
You're constantly re-writing."*

OKAY, you've reached the end. At least, the end of this phase: Your manuscript is finished.

Or is it?

You've run your manuscript past your beta readers. *(Principle #16)*

You've survived getting notes. *(Principle #17)*

You've gone through one or two (or three) rounds of "re-shooting." *(Principle #18)*

You've murdered your darlings. *(Principle #19)*

So, you're done with the writing (the post-production) phase, right?

Maybe.

This is the point where I take the advice of actor/director Bob Odenkirk (*Melvin Goes To Dinner, Better Call Saul*), who offered me some sage wisdom about moviemaking during our long phone conversation. And it's an idea which also completely applies to your current position.

"You've got to be patient once you hit the set," Odenkirk recommended. "You spend so much time preparing and hoping and working toward making a film. You can't get on the set and then hurry up and leave. You're there, the actors are there, the lights are there, the cameras are there, the set is there. It's all there. It's not going to be there again tomorrow.

"So don't hesitate to hesitate."

Wise words. Don't be afraid to stop and take time and take stock. Don't race onto the next thing.

Odenkirk recommends that you ask yourself: "What else could happen here? What else is really going on? And if there's anything that strikes you as needing to be there, see if you can get it. You're there. There's not going to be a better time to do it. So, make use of that opportunity."

Director Roger Nygard put it this way: "Every time you feel that the script is done, put it down for a week or a month, and then come back to it and you'll see that it's not done. Because it's never done. Writing is re-writing. You're constantly re-writing."

Don't hesitate to hesitate.

In short, I'm recommending that you take a short vacation from your book.

It's a healthy separation. Filmmakers do it all the time (when they can). The movie production process—long hours of writing, scouting, money-raising and pre-production, followed by weeks of grueling 18-hour days of shooting, followed by weeks or months of painstaking editing—can take a physical, emotional and creative toll on a filmmaker.

(Any of that feel familiar?)

During that process, you have to find ways to recharge your

batteries. For Darren Aronofsky, nothing does that better than taking a few hours off to see a movie.

His production diary for his film, *pi*, has one chapter entitled, Sometimes You Gotta Just Go See A Movie. In it, he notes: "I gave the editing crew the weekend off. After a fantastic push, the crew has earned it. We're all a bit exhausted, and a break is exactly what I needed. Today I will go see Woo's *Face-Off* and hopefully have a good time."

Steven Soderbergh agrees. While making *sex, lies and videotape*, on his one day off, he also took a break and went to see a movie.

Here's how he recorded it in his production journal: "Day off felt good. Saw *Tucker: The Man and His Dream*, which (I'd) been dying to see. Unfortunately, I was engaged aesthetically but not emotionally. It literally was one of the best designed and photographed films I've ever seen."

Getting outside of yourself is a smart way to recharge your creative energies and get you ready to dive back into the final phases of launching your book. And it's a method Soderbergh still uses to this day, although now he creates that space by working on several projects simultaneously.

He explained it to me this way: "I'm more and more finding ways to create pockets of time to step away, so that I can come back and be less precious. I think the biggest lesson I learned over the years is that preciousness—thinking too highly of your own material—is to be actively attacked. You come back to something and say, 'Oh my God, why is that in the film?'"

So, if you can, take time away. Step back from the book and work on (or think about) something else for a while.

How long? That's up to you. However, if you're not under contract and you're publishing your book yourself, time really is on your side. *(See Principle #24)*

BEYOND THE SCREEN QUESTIONS

- In what ways can you take a creative break from your writing?
- Once you're all refreshed and you look at your work again, are you willing to make the necessary changes to make it better? *(Principle #19)*

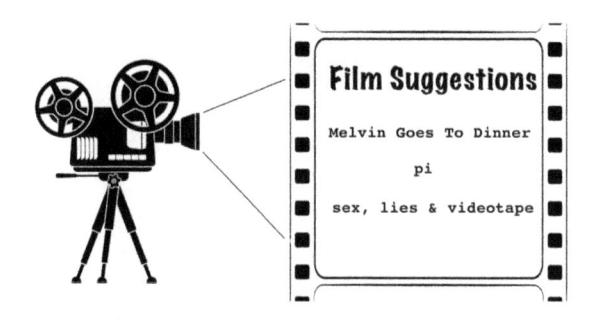

Film Suggestions

Melvin Goes To Dinner

pi

sex, lies & videotape

PART FOUR
DISTRIBUTION

Now it's time for the most hazardous step in your journey: Putting your work out into the real world.

PRINCIPLE #21
READ THE FINE PRINT

"I made a bad deal."

WHETHER YOU'RE WORKING with a big or small publishing house … or acting as your own publisher … you will be making agreements (contracts) with a surprising number of different parties along the way.

From publishing contracts, to agreements with your cover designer, to commitments made with distributors (i.e., Amazon's Kindle Publishing or ACX for audiobooks, and more), you will be adding your name and initials to some key contracts as you head toward publication.

The following should not in any sense be perceived as the do-all and end-all guide to the legalities of book publishing.

Instead, in each of the following horror stories, substitute the word "publisher" for each mention of the word "distributor," and you'll get a sense of your possible analogous experience in the book world.

It's hoped these dark tales will instill the idea that sound legal counsel should be employed when signing just about anything.

The legal lesson learned by the makers of *The Blair Witch Project* is a cautionary tale for anyone, regardless of the degree of success your project may (or may not) attain.

"We had this three-picture deal, post-*Blair Witch*, with Artisan that we thought was our guarantee to making movies into the decades to come," co-director Daniel Myrick told me. "And we found out that a lot of those so-called 'three picture deals' are just ways to leverage you later down the road. You effectively sign off the rights to your next two movies, which are two of your pet projects, to the distributor. And then they can, in turn, hold that as leverage to get you to do, or try to get you to do, *Blair 2*.

"That's a specific example of us learning a hard lesson. We signed off a couple of our best ideas because—in the heat of the moment—we thought our distributor was going to line them up and start making these movies with us. And then we came to find out that their primary interest was just making more *Blair* movies. And that wasn't where we wanted to go creatively at the time."

This same trap has snared novel writers as well: what seems like a sweet publishing deal actually locks you into a creative straitjacket which even Houdini would have trouble escaping.

In my own situation, when I 'signed' with a small, traditional publisher, I opted to not agree to their multi-book deal offer (which they were really pushing). I simply didn't want to be locked in, required to continue a series with them regardless of how the titles were selling. The downside was that I was always last on their publishing schedule. The upside was I was free to write what and when I wanted to. And also free to leave whenever I wanted to leave.

In the flush of excitement of being offered a much-anticipated 'book deal,' it's best to take a step back and ensure the terms are really something you can live with for a long, long time.

Because once you sign a contract, it's often very hard (and expensive) to un-sign it.

The following nightmare scenario involves (ironically) one of the great 'nightmare' movies ever conceived. Herk Harvey's *Carnival of Souls* was lost to us for a while, but then resurfaced as one of the most iconic low-budget horror films ever produced.

It was 'lost' due to some shoddy copyright work and the resulting confusion when the film's distributor went bankrupt.

However, before all that happened, the filmmakers were delighted to find a distributor at all.

"In the early days of independent productions, it was very hard to find anybody who would distribute a film. [Producer/director] Herk [Harvey] found this small distribution company," director of photography Maurice Prather recalled.

"We finally ended up with a distributor in California," Harvey explained. "We had high hopes for a return on our investment, which would enable us to produce more films."

Harvey signed the distribution papers and then took off to South America, to shoot a number of geography films for the company he worked for in Kansas.

"When I returned, I contacted the distributor," Harvey said. "They said, yes, they owed us money and that they would send us a check. When their check arrived, it bounced, and I knew we were in trouble. They were out of business."

With the distributor out of business, the lab that had made all the prints seized the film.

"The deal with the laboratories is if you don't pay for the product, it becomes their property," explained Prather. "And they can sell it to anybody they damn well please. That's what happened to Herk's film. The worst part was that the film was never copyrighted. We didn't know much about copyright laws."

Harvey realized his limitations too late. "It was a big mistake," he admitted. "At the time, we had all the experience necessary to produce films, but not the knowledge of the business end of distribution."

This, sadly, is true of many novel writers: They have all the talent to create books but lack the business acumen to ensure proper (and honest) distribution.

Looking back on it, Harvey had mixed feelings about the experience. "Making the film had been very exciting," he recalled. "Distributing the film had been agonizing. We bowed our heads and went back to our regular filmmaking activities."

The lab later sold the film to another lab, which then sold it for television broadcast, which was where this lost gem was eventually discovered by a new generation of film fans.

The experience of these newbie filmmakers—the sudden loss of their distribution company, their lack of knowledge about copyright—is a cautionary tale for all writers as they embark on the publication phase of their book's production.

And it raises questions you should be thinking about before you sign anything:

- What recourse do you have if your publisher goes under?
- What are the terms of the rights reversion clause in your contract? (that is, what will it take to get your rights back?)
- Who is copyrighting the book?
- Who owns the cover?
- Who owns the elements that make up the cover?

- What is the term length of your contract?
- For an audiobook, who pays the narrator?
- How long is the distribution term for your audiobook?
- How easy is it to change the terms of any contract?

The list goes on and on. And, sadly, even experienced people can make small mistakes in the contract phase, creating big headaches later on. As the next story demonstrates.

Writer/director/producer/actor Tom Noonan had been, on the whole, very happy with the process of making his first feature, *What Happened Was....*

Noonan—probably best known for his character work in films like *Manhunter, Synecdoche, New York, Last Action Hero* and *The Monster Squad*—had long wanted to create a low-budget film of his own.

From that desire came *What Happened Was....*

He had written and performed the two-person drama first as a play, working out all the performance kinks on-stage. When it came time to shoot it on the film's single set—a loft apartment somewhere in Manhattan—he did practice runs on video, to figure out shots and angles.

And then he shot the film and edited it.

It went on to be nominated for a couple of Independent Spirit awards and win two awards at the Sundance Film Festival (The Waldo Salt Screenwriting award and the Grand Jury prize).

However, Noonan's bliss with the project came to an abrupt halt when it came time to find distribution.

He experienced a myriad of problems—a bad contract that ultimately cost him more than it made him, a distributor who went through bankruptcy, a late video release, and a bad (and misleading) marketing campaign for the video.

Most damaging was a small clause in the distribution contract which ended up personally costing Noonan money every time the movie made any money.

"When you sell a film to a distributor, there's a certain aspect of the agreement that's called the assumption agreement," Noonan told me. "It's where the distributor agrees to assume certain costs involved in the distribution of the film, one of which is the residuals for the actors.

"Otherwise, if I sell you the film for $75,000 and I pay the crew and I pay everybody back, and then you go out and sell the film everywhere, the more money you make selling the film, the more money the actors have to get paid as residuals. And, unless the distributor assumes that expense, I end up losing money in the end making the film.

"When we made the agreement, I didn't know that and it was left out of the agreement, or somehow it didn't get signed. And I was left with the bill for the residuals. So besides not making any money, I lost money on the film."

Noonan, who is fairly well-versed in the ways of Hollywood, admits that he fell short in this area.

"Distribution is the creepiest part of making a movie, and there are so many ways you can get fucked in distribution. I had someone representing me, it wasn't just me, I had somebody who'd sold a lot of movies and they screwed up a little.

"I made a bad deal. But it's okay; I loved making the movie."

Like film distribution, book publication can—at times—be the creepiest part of the book creation process. You must always remember that everyone you meet throughout the book writing and releasing process DOES NOT necessarily have your best interests at heart. Read the fine print and sign contracts with care.

I'll close this section with a quote from filmmaker (and novelist) William Bayer.

As before, substitute the words "film industry" with "publishing industry," and the words "filmmaker" with "writer."

"The film industry is a zoo filled with wild animals. The young filmmaker is like a yearling deer wandering around among ruthless gorillas, vicious pigs, slippery lizards, scavenger hyenas, and carrion-eating jackals. The great difference between the zoo of the film industry and a real zoo is that in the zoo of the film industry there are no cages. BEWARE THE ANIMALS. They run wild and feed on the young filmmaker. The only law here is the law of the jungle."

BEYOND THE SCREEN QUESTIONS

- What contracts have you signed so far in your book writing journey? What have those contracts locked you into?
- Do you have contracts with vendors (cover designers, audiobook producers, editors) that clearly lay out the terms of the agreement?
- If you are signing with a publisher, do you understand the implications of that agreement and the impact it has on your rights?

Film Suggestions

The Blair Witch Project

Carnival of Souls

What Happened Was ...

PRINCIPLE #22
HIGH FIVES & HARSH WORDS: THE REVIEWS ARE IN

"There is only one sane way to deal with critics, and that is to ignore them."

SINCE WE CONCLUDED the last section with a quote from filmmaker and novelist William Bayer, it seems fitting to kick off this chapter with a few more wise words from him.

"There is only one sane way to deal with critics, and that is to ignore them," Bayer suggests. "Sure, appreciate their praise, and be grateful when it helps a picture and makes it possible to make another. But remember: if you believe them when they rave about you, you must also believe them when they pan you. And since they are human, and therefore prejudiced and fallible like anyone else, it is best to think of them as a necessary evil."

It's interesting to note that William Bayer started as a filmmaker and later moved into fiction writing, in part because he tired of the vagrancies of the film industry.

As he stated in the 1989 revision to his classic filmmaking book (*Breaking Through, Selling Out, Dropping Dead*), "Have I rejected cinema? As an art form, certainly not. As a lifestyle, most decidedly yes ... I [now] go quietly about my work creating imaginary worlds, peopled by imaginary characters, using language instead of images, beholden to no one."

Of course, as a novelist, Bayer (and all of us) must decide how we approach and react to reviews.

Some writers never read them, end of story. (Or so they claim.)

Others avidly read each one, scanning Amazon for fluctuations in their star rating and parsing each new review like a long-lost Dead Sea scroll.

I think most of us fall somewhere in the middle.

It's a good idea to scan reviews occasionally, particularly right after a new book's release. This is to determine if we are marketing it to the correct audience.

If, for example, cozy readers are objecting to the sex and violence in your story, you've somehow marketed the book to the wrong audience and must correct the error. It might be the blurb, it might be the cover, but something is giving potential readers the wrong idea about your book.

In short, the wrong readers are buying it and expressing their displeasure at something which wasn't intended for them in the first place.

Those are reviews worth noting. You should take swift action to correct the marketing mistakes and make sure your book is being targeted to (and reviewed by) the right audience.

Other than that issue, reviews are always going to vary. You can't please everyone, nor should you try.

As director Mike Nichols observed of his own work: "The things I've done are neither as good as the people who carry on say they are, nor are they as bad as the reaction to the reaction says they are. They're just sort of in-between."

So, other than making sure your book is finding the right audience, on the whole I think it's best to ignore reviews.

That time is better spent writing your next book.

BEYOND THE SCREEN QUESTIONS

- Do you seek out and read reviews of your work?
- Have you ever responded to a review?
- Do you think responding is a good or bad idea?

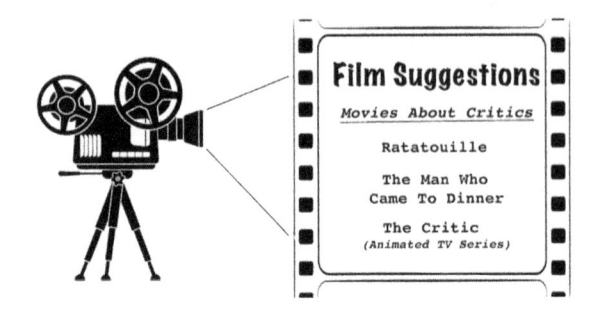

Film Suggestions

Movies About Critics

Ratatouille

The Man Who Came To Dinner

The Critic
(Animated TV Series)

PRINCIPLE #23
NEVER NEED HOLLYWOOD

*"The less you need them,
the happier you're gonna be."*

FILMMAKERS HAVE RAILED against Hollywood for years. Probably since the beginning of Hollywood.

Fiction writers have felt a similar conflict with their industry's "powers that be" — that is, agents and editors and publishers who appear to stand between you and getting your book published.

But times have (finally) changed.

Just as the need for Hollywood has diminished over the years, so too has the need to deal with the publishing establishment.

In short: You don't need them to get your book out into the world.

Independent filmmakers have known this (and profited from it) for years.

Here are a few significant examples which might inspire you

to set your own course with your book. Just substitute the words "Hollywood" for "Publishers" and you'll be on your way.

Filmmaker Henry Jaglom *(Someone To Love, Venice/Venice, A Safe Place)* was great friends with the director Orson Welles, from whom he learned this key lesson: Never need Hollywood.

"Never depend on it for your financing, for support, for your ability to make films," Jaglom told me. "Get your backing as far away as possible from what they proudly call their 'Industry' if you have any intention of being an artist. The less you need them, the happier you're gonna be.

"Co-existence cannot occur, as Orson's last two decades sadly showed," Jaglom explained. "He needed them till the end, and they rejected him till the end. And a half-dozen or more brilliant motion pictures never got made as a result. And a magnificent artist could never get back to the canvas that they had pulled out from under him."

Unlike filmmakers of past eras, Jaglom believes today's filmmaker is in a perfect position to avoid all the traps and trappings of Hollywood.

"This is a great time to be an independent filmmaker," he said. "There are more venues than ever before, there's a bigger, ever-growing audience, there's an ever-growing economic system to support it, there are endless distribution opportunities. It is the best time to be a truly independent filmmaker."

The same is absolutely true for writers and the books they want to create. All the tools are available for you right now, from ideation all the way through self-distribution.

Going your own way can be harder, of course, because you're on your own. But it has many pluses as well.

Writer/director Dan O'Bannon (*Dark Star, Alien, Return of the Living Dead*) feels that working at the low-budget level of *Dark Star* had many advantages over the higher-budget films he subsequently was involved in as a writer or director.

"One of the advantages to having no money is that you could do anything you want," he said. "You don't have some asshole standing there, saying 'We want a re-write.' Or, 'That's in bad taste,' or 'We've been talking it over, and we think you should...' No. Fuck you.

"[On Dark Star,] John [Carpenter] and I wrote a scene, and if we both liked it we went out and shot it," O'Bannon continued. "In that regard it beat all subsequent filmmaking hands down. You could just do what you wanted to do. It may have been hard, and you may not have had resources and it was a challenge, but you didn't have some butthole sitting on your back like Sinbad's Old Man of the Sea, with his arms and legs wrapped around your head, telling you how to ruin your film."

Filmmaker Eric Mendelson agreed with that sentiment. In fact, it was part of his ethos while making *Judy Berlin*.

"People were offering us a lot of money to make [*Judy Berlin*] at a higher budget," Mendelson recalled. "However, the low budget was a way for me to maintain control."

Mendelsohn learned during the financing stage of pre-production that whenever outside producers offered to finance the film for more money, they also wanted to change elements that he was unwilling to alter.

"They wanted to make the film at a higher budget, but could

we get rid of Madeline Kahn? They wanted to make it at a higher budget, but could Judy Berlin be played by such and such a Hollywood star? But when you have nothing, nobody cares about you and that's great. So, I had control with my little budget, I had absolute control."

The benefits of that low budget were not wasted on the film's leading lady, Edie Falco *(The Sopranos, Nurse Jackie)*, who has found the atmosphere on low-budget productions to be often more conducive to creative results.

"There are so many advantages to working on a low-budget project," Falco told me. "I feel totally comfortable with the idea of trying something and having it not work. I feel a sense of freedom to just go for it, because money is not at the forefront of everything that goes on with these things. You don't have a producer standing over you saying, 'We gotta make the day!'

"Everybody's just flying by the seat of their pants, and I feel a sense of freedom that I don't when money is being talked about. It's been my experience that nothing but good stuff will come out of that."

While many filmmakers long to leave their low-budget, non-Hollywood days behind them, there is a downside to success.

When Steven Soderbergh made *sex, lies and videotape,* he never expected the nearly universal acclaim the film ultimately received. The fact was, Soderbergh had less than high hopes when he started the project. He considered it as "a feature-length resume piece that would get me a job making a real movie," he said.

While that perspective may seem negative, it actually had the opposite effect. With so few expectations, everyone was able to experiment and take some creative chances.

"The great thing about [*sex, lies and videotape*] was that all of us felt pretty free to do whatever occurred to us," Soderbergh told me. "There was no pressure and you felt like no one was watching you."

So, in spite of the low budget and the relatively quick 30-day shooting schedule, he felt he had more control than he would later experience with larger productions.

"On that movie, I felt I had more time to do the work than I have had since on any movie," Soderbergh said. "That was the only movie where I never once felt rushed and felt like I had all the time I needed to do the work on a given day. And every film since then, I've felt like I didn't have enough time.

"*Out of Sight* cost $49 million," he continued. "And every day you felt like you had a gun to your head."

BEYOND THE SCREEN QUESTIONS

- Are you free of the constraints of the publishing industry or do you need to work within the system to achieve your goals?
- What benefits are you experiencing by being free of the publishing industry?
- What are you willing to give up in order to be taken in by the industry (if that's what you want)?

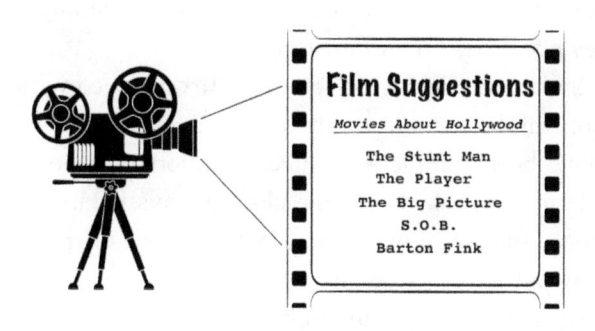

Film Suggestions
Movies About Hollywood

The Stunt Man
The Player
The Big Picture
S.O.B.
Barton Fink

PRINCIPLE #24
TIME IS ON YOUR SIDE

*"What we lacked in monetary
resources, we had in time."*

HERE'S something that's easy to forget in the mad whirlwind to write / finish / publish your book: Unless you're under a contracted deadline, time is on your side. You can take all the time you need to finish your book (and your cover and your blurb), to get all the elements just right.

The lack of time is very often a significant factor in shooting and releasing movies, but there are examples when filmmakers have used the freedom independence brings to literally take the time they need to get their movie right.

For the low-budget sci-fi classic, *Dark Star*, co-writer Dan O'Bannon thinks without the luxury of time, the movie would never have been completed. Unlike traditional movies—with a cast and crew on salary and the clock always ticking away on equipment and location fees—director John Carpenter and O'Bannon used their student status (and the exceptional film resources) at USC to make their film at a relatively leisurely pace.

"The only thing that made it possible with the small amount of money we had is that we would shoot for a few days, then we would stop for a couple weeks while we scraped together enough resources and money to shoot another scene or two," O'Bannon told me. "If we hadn't had those long time gaps, I don't think we could have done that picture on that budget."

Similarly, director David Lynch took his own sweet time to make his early effort. To be more specific, about four years.

The original shooting schedule for *Eraserhead* was pretty typical.

"It was supposed to take a few weeks to shoot," explained assistant director Catherine Coulson (who later turned up as The Log Lady on *Twin Peaks*). "I think the original shooting schedule was six weeks."

That six weeks stretched on ... and on ... and on.

"After a film's going for a couple of years, you sort of find your rhythm," Lynch said. "We normally did about one shot a night. A 'master shot' would definitely be lighting all night."

There were certain benefits to such a leisurely schedule.

"What we lacked in monetary resources, we had in time," recalled Director of Photography Fred Elmes. "We could take the time to build something right. We could shoot a test, and if it didn't look right, we'd go back to the drawing board and build it again."

The downside to such a long schedule were issues like maintaining vision and energy, and dealing with minor problems, like continuity.

"There's one particular shot, when Henry (actor Jack Nance) walks down the hall," Lynch recalled. "He puts his hand on the doorknob and turns it, and there's a cut. A year and a half later he comes through the door! Those things can be extremely frightening, to think about holding a mood and a correctness, something that will stick together after four years. It's pretty hard."

Lynch continued: "There were some dark moments. At one

time I was thinking about building a small eight-inch Henry and stop-motioning him through some small cardboard sets to fill in the blanks. Just to get it finished."

"It just turned into this monster we couldn't finish," Nance said. "It was a killer, but Lynch wouldn't give it up. We couldn't give it up. So, we kept shooting."

Although he was happy with the final result, in retrospect Lynch felt that four years was just too long to devote to one movie.

"I feel now that I shouldn't have spent so much time on *Eraserhead*," he admitted. "I should like to have made more films in that time, but it wasn't happening. I couldn't do anything new, because *Eraserhead* wasn't finished. I didn't have anything to show anybody. So, I just saw the world going by and tried to raise money and, little by little, I did it.

"The thing is, the film isn't done until it's done."

Filmmaker Eric Mendelsohn didn't have much money to work with, but he did have something of equal or greater value – time. He could take all the time he wanted to plan out the shooting of his film, *Judy Berlin*, in meticulous detail.

"I worked on films my whole life and I have been a crew member my whole life. So I knew every trick," Mendelsohn explained. "I knew what we needed was pre-production. It was put together like a little army. It wasn't just knowing where we were headed every day; we also had at least two fallback positions for everything. This was months and months and months of pre-production."

Mendelsohn recommends taking the time you need to get things right—especially when that time isn't costing you anything.

"It's sort of unheard of, but I knew that if you don't have

money and you don't have any more manpower than anyone else has, you need time," he reasoned. "So, I just kept adding in pre-production time, because that was something I could afford."

The same was true for Chris Kentis and his film, *Open Water*.

Because he was financing the low-budget movie with his own money, he wasn't beholden to anyone else's arbitrary schedule. That was just one of several advantages to his approach.

"The first advantage of taking our time was that I was able to work full time and help finance the film," Kentis explained. "Another is that movies tend to be rushed, especially if you look at the things coming out of Hollywood today. I think there's a lot to be said for taking the time to get it right, and I think most films don't really have that advantage. It's a process of refinement.

"You write the script, and you're going to write at least ten drafts of a script," he continued. "And just when you think you can't possibly have it more concise and more economical, then you shoot the thing, and you can't believe how much fat there was on it. And it's the same thing when you go through the editing process.

"When you're making a film like this, without a crew, lack of objectivity can be a real problem, so having the time to step back and get some distance is really critical."

There's no question that eliminating time as a factor can remove a lot of pressure on you as you create your book.

Filmmaker Tom Noonan realized that while he wrote, produced, directed and acted in his wonderful feature, *What Happened Was …*

"One thing I learned making the film, is that you have a huge advantage when you have no money, because when you have no money you have all the time in the world," Noonan explained.

"The more money you have, the less time you have to make a film, because you've got to move or you're wasting money. So, if you're smart and you're talented and skillful and you manage your time well, you can actually do a whole lot better movie with very little money than you can with tons. Because once tons of money gets involved, you have millions of people trying to put their finger in the pie and tell you what to do and rush you along.

"And I never had that. I wrote this at the pace I wanted to, I shot it when I felt like it, and I edited it for as long as I wanted."

BEYOND THE SCREEN QUESTIONS

- Are you being pressured by imaginary time constraints?
- What benefits can you see slowing down and taking your time might bring?

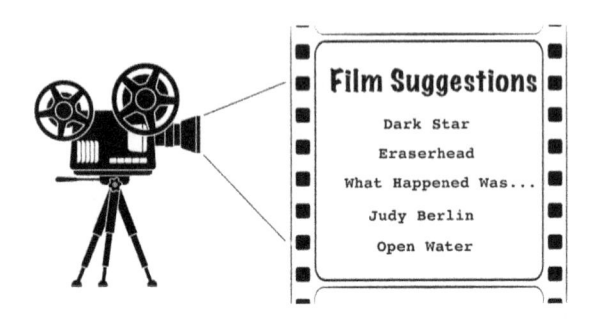

Film Suggestions

Dark Star
Eraserhead
What Happened Was...
Judy Berlin
Open Water

PRINCIPLE #25
THE BEST ADVICE

AND, finally, the best advice of all.

There's one simple step you can take to help you succeed in your work.

While all the principles in this book are valuable (and a few I would even call invaluable), this one supersedes them all.

I'm quoting from a conversation with Eric Bogosian *(Talk Radio, subUrbia)* here, but this could have been said by any creative person quoted in this book.

And it's simply this: *"Keep writing."*

That's the alpha and the omega. The beginning and the end.

Just keep doing that and you'll be fine.

AFTERWORD

We've reached the end of the story, at least for now.

If you've gathered nothing else from these principles, I hope it's the understanding that in fiction writing (as in moviemaking), there really is no one right or wrong way. There are only stories that work and those that don't. And processes that work for you. And those that don't.

My advice? Worry less about formulas and more about the heart you need to bring to your writing. If you're passionate about your tale, and have the skill and drive to tell it well, then I say onward and upward!

Think about each of the twenty-five filmmaking principles we've just discussed and keep asking yourself: What's my version of that? How can that idea help me move forward?

Finally, I'll say this: if you take nothing else away from this book, at the very least embrace *Principle #1: Stop Getting Ready and Just Do It!* Nothing happens until you get over that first hump. So start writing. Keep writing. Keep reading. Keep pondering. And keep in touch.

John Gaspard
www.albertsbridgebooks.com

GET YOUR FREE ELI MARKS SHORT STORY BUNDLE

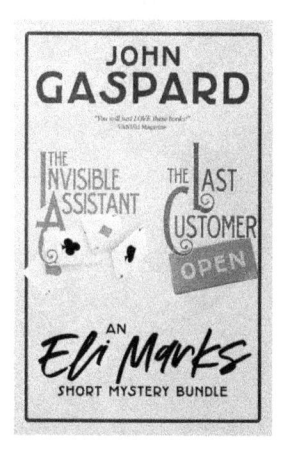

The Eli Marks Short Mystery Bundle
"The Invisible Assistant" & "The Last Customer"
Two short-story cozy mysteries in one!

"You will just LOVE these books." – VANISH Magazine

The Invisible Assistant
There's no question it was murder. But who killed whom?
What begins as a typical corporate event for magician Eli

Marks turns into a twisted mystery when he is called to the site of a recent murder/suicide. Confronted by the details of the grisly crime scene, Eli must sort through the post-mortem clues - and the bickering of the officials as well as a poorly-timed allergy attack - to determine just who murdered whom.

The Last Customer

The request was a first for Eli Marks: "Can you help me make my tuba disappear?"

Magician (and magic shop owner) Eli Marks is confronted with this odd demand just before he is about to close up shop for the day. Over the next few tense minutes, he finds a solution to that question which also, fortunately, puts him the positive side of what turns out to be a life-or-death situation.

Go to www.elimarksmysteries.com

GET YOUR FREE COMO LAKE PLAYERS SHORT MYSTERY

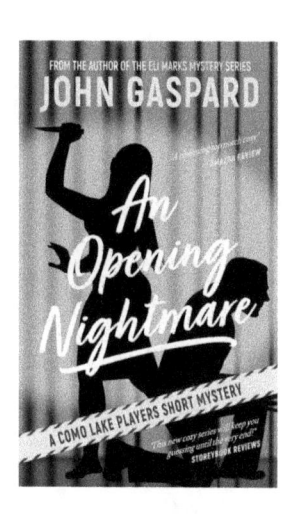

An Opening Nightmare

A Como Lake Players Short Mystery

A Killer Show, With the Corpses To Prove It

When an audience member is stabbed in the middle of an Opening Night performance, Leah must figure out who this clever killer is ... and make sure they don't kill the run of her show! Or murder her, as well!

A great introduction to The Como Lake Players mystery series: New Executive Director (and former actress) Leah Sexton must navigate the twisty world of community theater while dealing with crazy Board members, egomaniacal directors, self-centered actors ... and the occasional cold-blooded killer.

"This new cozy series will keep you guessing until the very end!" — Storeybook Reviews

Go to: https://www.albertsbridgebooks.com

JOIN THE NEWSLETTER

Keep in touch about all the books at Albert's Bridge books — The Como Lake Players mysteries ... the Eli Marks mysteries ... plus occasional deals on other mysteries, as well as film and writing books! And no spam!

Go to: https://www.albertsbridgebooks.com

ABOUT THE AUTHOR

John is author of the Eli Marks mystery series as well as four other stand-alone novels, *"The Sword & Mr. Stone," "A Christmas Carl," "The Greyhound of the Baskervilles"* and *"The Ripperologists."*

He also writes the *Como Lake Players* mystery series.

In real life, John's not a magician, but he has directed six low-budget features that cost very little and made even less—that's no small trick.

He's also written books on the subject of low-budget film-making. Ironically, they've made more than the films. Those books (*"Fast, Cheap and Under Control"* and *"Fast, Cheap and Written That Way"*) are available in eBook, Paperback and audio-book formats.

John lives in Minnesota and shares his home with his lovely wife, several dogs, a few cats and a handful of pet allergies.

Find out more at: https://www.albertsbridgebooks.com and https://www.elimarksmysteries.com.

- facebook.com/JohnGaspardAuthorPage
- twitter.com/johngaspard
- instagram.com/johngaspard
- bookbub.com/authors/john-gaspard

BOOKS BY JOHN GASPARD

The Como Lake Players Mysteries
ACTING CAN BE MURDER
DYING TO AUDITION
REHEARSED TO DEATH
AN OPENING NIGHTMARE (Novella)

The Eli Marks Mystery Series
THE AMBITIOUS CARD (#1)
THE BULLET CATCH (#2)
THE MISER'S DREAM (#3)
THE LINKING RINGS (#4)
THE FLOATING LIGHT BULB (#5)
THE ZOMBIE BALL (#6)
THE MAGIC SQUARE (#7)
THE SELF-WORKING TRICK (#8)

Stand-Alone Novels
THE SWORD & MR. STONE
A CHRISTMAS CARL
THE GREYHOUND OF THE BASKERVILLES
THE RIPPEROLOGISTS

Filmmaking & Writing Books
THE POPCORN PRINCIPLES
FAST, CHEAP AND UNDER CONTROL
FAST, CHEAP AND WRITTEN THAT WAY
TELL THEM IT'S A DREAM SEQUENCE
WOMEN MAKE MOVIES

NOTES

ALL THE QUOTES in the book—with the exception of the following citations—were taken from interviews conducted by the author for the books *"Fast Cheap and Under Control," "Fast Cheap and Written That Way," "Tell Them It's a Dream Sequence,"* and *"Women Make Movies."*

PRINCIPLE #1: STOP GETTING READY AND JUST DO IT

"To 'try' is to struggle in a powerless situation..." Noonan, Tom, *www.tomnoonan.com*

"I went for hands-on, technical stuff..." Smith, Kevin, *An Evening With Kevin Smith*, DVD

"I was inventing my own film school ..." Rodriguez, Robert, *Rebel Without a Crew*, Plume, 1996

PRINCIPLE #2: READ. WRITE. REPEAT

"If you don't have the time to read ..." King, Stephen, *On Writing: A Memoir of the Craft*, Scribner, 2000

• • •

PRINCIPLE #3: EXPLOIT THE UNIQUE

"It was sunset and I was driving back to Kansas ..." Harvey, Herk, *Carnival of Souls* DVD Commentary

"When I got back to Kansas ..." Harvey, Herk, *Carnival of Souls* DVD Commentary

"You create what you observe, what you see around you ..." Engel, Joel, *Screenwriters on Screenwriting,* MJF Books, 1995

"Readers are interested in the way a writer sees things ..." Fforde, Jasper, *"Pep Talk From Jasper Fforde,"* https://nanowrimo.org/pep-talk-from-jasper-fforde

PRINCIPLE #5: YOU GOTTA BE COMMITTED

"We were dealing with a fantasy premise..." Russo, John, *The Complete Night of the Living Dead Filmbook*, page 73

"Having made sure that you accepted the rules ..." Thompson, David, *Demme on Demme, Part 2: Caged Heat to Fighting Mad*

PRINCIPLE #6: COME IN LATE, LEAVE EARLY

"You always attack a movie scene as late ..." Meyers, Scott, *"Writing Mantra: Enter late, Exit Early,"* https://scottdistillery.medium.com/writing-mantra-enter-late-exit-early-45a9060bdf7b

"I want people to get the feeling that they're being dropped ..." Engel, Joel, *Screenwriters on Screenwriting,* MJF Books, 1995

"The material shot in Liebkind's apartment ..." Rosenblum, Ralph, and Karen, Robert, *"When the Shooting Stops...the Cutting Begins,"* 1979

"That's where you want to cut ..." Rosenblum, Ralph, and Karen, Robert, *"When the Shooting Stops...the Cutting Begins,"* 1979

PRINCIPLE #7: CUTTING THE SHOE LEATHER

"The walk from here to there is not interesting ..." Nygard,

Roger, *"Cut To The Monkey: A Hollywood Editor's Behind-the-Scenes Secrets to Making Hit Comedies,"* 2021

"Originally, there were a series of long scenes ..." Pollack, Sydney, *Tootsie Criterion Collection*, 1991

"Leave out the parts that readers tend to skip ..." Leonard, Elmore, *"Elmore Leonard's Ten Rules of Writing,"* 2007

PRINCIPLE #8: INTENTIONS & OBSTACLES

"I kind of worship at the altar of intention ..." Sorkin, Aaron, *Esquire Magazine*, December 2010

"If you can't break a dramatic scene down ..." Badham, John, *"I'll Be in My Trailer,"* Michael Wiese Productions, 2006

"A movie script has to have conflict ..." Engel, Joel, *Screenwriters on Screenwriting*, MJF Books, 1995

PRINCIPLE #9: DON'T SPILL ALL YOUR POPCORN IN THE LOBBY

"Any good movie is filled with secrets ..." Bose, Swapnil Dhruv, *Far Out Magazine*, https://faroutmagazine.co.uk/mike-nichols-coming-of-age-drama-the-graduate/

"We were a few days into shooting the pilot ..." Sorkin, Aaron, "The West Wing Weekly Podcast"

PRINCIPLE #10: SAVE THE CAT, KILL THE CAT.

"Harpo, in the first scene of *A Night at the Opera* ..." Steinberg, David, "The Marx Brothers in a Nutshell," 1982

PRINCIPLE #11: CALLBACKS

"Julius Epstein has always said that the ending ..." Harmetz, Aljean, *"Round Up the Usual Suspects: The Making of 'Casablanca'—Bogart, Bergman, and World War II,"* Hyperion, 1992, Page 230

"Audiences love a callback ..." Scheinert, Daniel, *IndieWire's Filmmaker Toolkit Podcast*, December 9, 2022.

PRINCIPLE #12: GREAT EXPOSITION

"We interrupt our programme for a special police message..." Stoppard, Tom, *"The Real Inspector Hound,"* Grove Press, 1968

"Hello, the drawing-room of Lady Muldoon's ..." Stoppard, Tom, *"The Real Inspector Hound,"* Grove Press, 1968

"When you have a lot of characters in a movie ..." Sayles, John, *Return of the Secaucus 7*, DVD Commentary

"Exposition—every movie has it ..." Jenkins, Richard, *"Fresh Air,"* https://www.keranews.org/2018-02-21/actor-richard-jenkins-reading-shape-of-water-script-was-a-holy-mackerel-moment

PRINCIPLE #14: KEEP LESTER AWAKE

"My first goal is not to bore anybody ..." Levant, Brian, *"The Marx Brothers Council Podcast,"* December 17, 2022

PRINCIPLE #15: ALL'S WELL THAT ENDS WELL

"I thought the script was funny ..." Muir, John Kenneth, *"An Askew View: The Films of Kevin Smith,"* Applause Books, 2002

"To me it was like, that's the ultimate joke ..." Lowenstein, Stephen, *"My First Movie 20 Celebrated Directors Talk About Their First Film,"* Penguin Books, 2002

"Right before we went to Sundance ..." Lowenstein, Stephen, *"My First Movie 20 Celebrated Directors Talk About Their First Film,"* Penguin Books, 2002

"I felt that it was truer to the story that Chad ..." *London Student*, Vol. 18, Issue 10

. . .

PRINCIPLE #16: PREVIEWS!

"Michael and I (stepped out) to get some popcorn ..." Culture Mix Online, *Spinal Tap 35th Anniversary Reunion*, https://culturemixonline.com/spinal-tap-director-rob-reiner-reunite-celebrate-35th-anniversary-spinal-tap/

"For a comedy person, it's a must ..." *"Putting Films To The Test,"* The New York Times, June 25, 2000

https://www.nytimes.com/2000/06/25/movies/film-putting-films-to-the-test-every-time.html

"You can't really know what your film is saying ..." Howard Ron, *"Grand Theft Auto,"* DVD Commentary

"Funny is funny ..." Howard Ron, *"Grand Theft Auto,"* DVD Commentary

"The first showing of Holy Grail was a total ..." The Pythons (with Bob McCabe), *The Pythons Autobiography*, page 263

"It was a disaster, an absolute disaster ..." Eggers, Dave, *"Sixteen Tons of Fun: Eric Idle brings the Holy Grail to Broadway,"* The New Yorker, December 20 & 27, 2004, page 171

"It was one of those evenings when Python flopped ..." The Pythons (with Bob McCabe), *The Pythons Autobiography*, page 263

"What had happened was ..." Morgan, David, and Olive, John, *Monty Python Speaks!*, Dey Street Books, 2019

"There were thirteen screenings of Holy Grail ..." The Pythons (with Bob McCabe), *The Pythons Autobiography*, page 264

PRINCIPLE #17: GETTING NOTES

Maximum Entertainment 2.0 — Weber, Ken, "Maximum Entertainment 2.0," https://www.max-ent.info

PRINCIPLE #18: THERE IS NO SHAME IN RESHOOTING

"Part of my strategy for shooting this film ..." Liman, Doug, *Swingers*, DVD Commentary

"We ended up scheduling 18 of the days ..." Liman, Doug, *Swingers* DVD: *"Making it in Hollywood"* Documentary

"The movie wouldn't be the movie that it became ..." Liman, Doug, *Swingers* DVD: *"Making it in Hollywood"* Documentary

"I could see the flaws in *Shadows* myself ..." Carney, Ray, *"Cassavetes on Cassavetes,"* Farrar, Straus and Giroux, 2001

"The one thing that came to me after ..." Carney, Ray, *"Cassavetes on Cassavetes,"* Farrar, Straus and Giroux, 2001

"We started again, and I tried to shoot it ..." Carney, Ray, *"Cassavetes on Cassavetes,"* Farrar, Straus and Giroux, 2001

"The second version is completely different ..." Carney, Ray, *"Cassavetes on Cassavetes,"* Farrar, Straus and Giroux, 2001

PRINCIPLE #19: KILL YOUR DARLINGS

"Kill your darlings, kill your darlings ..." King, Stephen, *"On Writing: A Memoir of the Craft,"* Scribner, 2000

"We knew it was different, and a risk ... " Corliss, Richard, *"Blair Witch Craft,"* Time, August 16, 1999

"The pacing is slow in *Eraserhead,* and that's great ... " *Eraserhead: The Story Behind The Strangest Film Ever Made, And The Cinematic Genius Who Directed It, "Cinefantastique,* September, 1984, Vol 14 No 4 / Vol 14 No 5, pages 67-68

"After that screening, I drove over to ..." Rodley, Chris, *Lynch on Lynch,* Farrar, Straus and Giroux, 2005

"I always try to look at a completed film ..." Gelmiş, Joseph, *The Film Director as Superstar,* Doubleday, 1970

"We don't know what will happen to them ..." Leigh Jennifer Jason, *The Anniversary Party,* DVD Commentary

"You are very likely to vest what you've written ..." Engel, Joel, *Screenwriters on Screenwriting,* MJF Books, 1995

PRINCIPLE #20: DON'T HESITATE TO HESITATE

"I gave the editing crew the weekend off ..." Aronofsky, Darren, "*Pi, The Guerilla Diaries*," Faber & Faber, 1999

"Day off felt good ..." Soderbergh, Steven, "*sex, lies and videotape*" *(script and journal)*, Harper Collins, 1990

PRINCIPLE #21: READ THE FINE PRINT

"In the early days of independent productions ..." Lybarger, Dan, *Digital Souls: An Interview with Maurice Prather on Carnival of Souls*, February 3, 2000. Originally appeared in the February 3-9, 2000 issue of *Pitch Weekly*

"We finally ended up with a distributor in California ..." Harvey, Herk, *Carnival of Souls* DVD Commentary

"When I returned, I contacted the distributor ..." Harvey, Herk, *Carnival of Souls* DVD Commentary

"The deal with the laboratories is if you don't pay ..." Lybarger, Dan, *Digital Souls: An Interview with Maurice Prather on Carnival of Souls*, February 3, 2000. Originally appeared in the February 3-9, 2000 issue of *Pitch Weekly*

"It was a big mistake ..." Frentzen, Jeff, "*Herk Harvey's Carnival of Souls*," *Cinefantastique*, Vol 13 No 6 / Vol 14 No 1

"Making the film had been very exciting ..." Harvey, Herk, *Carnival of Souls* DVD Commentary

"The film industry is a zoo filled with wild animals ..." Bayer, William, "*Breaking Through, Selling Out, Dropping Dead and Other Notes on Filmmaking*," Limelight Editions, 1971, 1989.

PRINCIPLE #22: HIGH FIVES & HARSH WORDS: THE REVIEWS ARE IN

"There is only one sane way to deal with critics ..." Bayer, William, "*Breaking Through, Selling Out, Dropping Dead and Other Notes on Filmmaking*," Limelight Editions, 1971, 1989.

"Have I rejected cinema? As an art form ..." Bayer, William,

"Breaking Through, Selling Out, Dropping Dead and Other Notes on Filmmaking," Limelight Editions, 1971, 1989.

"The things I've done are neither as good ..." Gelmiş, Joseph, *The Film Director as Superstar,* Doubleday, 1970

PRINCIPLE #23: NEVER NEED HOLLYWOOD

"Co-existence cannot occur ..." Jaglom, Henry, *"Lessons From Orson," Moviemaker,* Issue No. 10, November 1994

"This is a great time to be an independent filmmaker ..." Jaglom, Henry, *"The Independent's Independent," Moviemaker,* Issue No. 14, July/August 1995, page 45

"A feature-length resume piece ..." Soderbergh, Steven, *sex, lies and videotape,* DVD Commentary

"Out of Sight cost $49 million ..." Soderbergh, Steven, *sex, lies and videotape,* DVD Commentary

PRINCIPLE #24: TIME IS ON YOUR SIDE

"It was supposed to take a few weeks to shoot ..." Godwin, K. George, *"Eraserhead: The Story Behind The Strangest Film Ever Made, And The Cinematic Genius Who Directed It, "Cinefantastique,* September 1984, Vol 14 No 4 / Vol 14 No 5, page 50

"After a film's going for a couple of years ..." Hughes, David, *The Complete Lynch,* Virgin Pub, 2001

"What we lacked in monetary resources ..." Godwin, K. George, *"Eraserhead: The Story Behind The Strangest Film Ever Made, And The Cinematic Genius Who Directed It, "Cinefantastique,* September 1984, Vol 14 No 4 / Vol 14 No 5, page 66

"There's one particular shot ..." Lynch, David, *Eraserhead,* DVD Commentary

"Those things can be extremely frightening ..." Rodley, Chris, *Lynch on Lynch,* Farrar, Straus and Giroux, 2005

"There were some dark moments ..." Alexander, John, *The Films of David Lynch,* page 43

"It just turned into this monster we couldn't finish ..." Hughes, David, *The Complete Lynch*, Virgin Pub, 2001

"I feel now that I shouldn't have spent so much time ..." Rodley, Chris, *Lynch on Lynch*, Farrar, Straus and Giroux, 2005

"The thing is, the film isn't done until it's done ..." Godwin, K. George, "*Eraserhead: The Story Behind The Strangest Film Ever Made, And The Cinematic Genius Who Directed It,* "*Cinefantastique*, September, 1984, Vol 14 No 4 / Vol 14 No 5, page 55)

FILMOGRAPHY

Adaptation
Dir. Spike Jonze
Columbia Pictures, 2002

After Hours
Dir. Martin Scorsese
Warner Bros., 1985

The Anniversary Party
Dir. Alan Cumming / Jennifer Jason Leigh
New Line, 2001

Back to the Future
Dir. Robert Zemeckis
Universal, 1985

Barton Fink
Dir. Joel Coen
20th Century Fox, 1991

The Big Chill
Dir. Lawrence Kasdan
Columbia Pictures, 1983

The Big Picture
Dir. Christopher Guest
Columbia Pictures, 1989

The Blair Witch Project
Dir. Daniel Myrick / Eduardo Sánchez
Artisan Entertainment, 1999

Butch Cassidy and The Sundance Kid
Dir. George Roy Hill
20th Century Fox, 1969

Caged Heat
Dir. Jonathan Demme
New World Pictures, 1974

Can You Ever Forgive Me
Dir. Marielle Heller
Searchlight Pictures, 2018

Capote
Dir. Bennett Miller
MGM Studios, 2005

Carnival of Souls
Dir. Herk Harvey
Harcourt Productions, 1962

Casablanca
Dir. Michael Curtiz
Warner Bros., 1942

Clerks
Dir. Kevin Smith
Miramax, 1994

The Critic
Created by Al Jean and Mike Reiss
Columbia Pictures Television, 1994-2001

Dark Star
Dir. John Carpenter
Jack H. Harris Enterprises, 1974

David Holzman's Diary
Dir. Jim McBride
Lorber Films, 1967

El Mariachi
Dir. Robert Rodriguez
Columbia Pictures, 1992

The End of the Tour
Dir. James Ponsoldt
A24, 2015

Eraserhead
Dir. David Lynch
Libra Films, 1977

From Dusk Till Dawn
Dir. Robert Rodriguez
Dimension Films, 1996

Gambit
Dir. Ronald Neame
Universal, 1966

Go
Dir. Doug Liman
Columbia Pictures, 1999

Hester Street
Dir. Joan Micklin Silver
Midwest Films, 1975

In the Company of Men
Dir. Neil LaBute
Sony Pictures Classics, 1997

Judy Berlin
Dir. Eric Mendelsohn
Image Entertainment, 1999

Jurassic Park
Dir. Steven Spielberg
Universal Pictures, 1993

The Last Broadcast
Dir. Stefan Avalos / Lance Weiler
101 Films, 1998

Living in Oblivion
Dir. Tom DiCillo
Columbia TriStar Home Video, 1995

The Man Who Came To Dinner
Dir. William Keighley
Warner Bros., 1942

Martin
Dir. George Romero
Laurel Productions, 1976

Me and You and Everyone We Know
Dir. Miranda July
IFC Films, 2005

Melvin Goes to Dinner
Dir. Bob Odenkirk
Arrival Pictures, 2003

Metropolitan
Dir. Whit Stillman
New Line Cinema, 1990

Monty Python and the Holy Grail
Dir. Terry Gilliam / Terry Jones
Python (Monty) Pictures, 1975

A Night at the Opera
Dir. Sam Wood
MGM, 1935

Night of the Living Dead
Dir. George Romero
Image Ten, 1968

Open Water
Dir. Chris Kentis
Lions Gate Films, 2003

pi
Dir. Darren Aronofsky
Harvest Filmworks, 1998

The Player
Dir. Robert Altman
Avenue Pictures, 1992

The Producers
Dir. Mel Brooks
Embassy Pictures, 1967

Ratatouille
Dir. Brad Bird / Jan Pinkava
Walt Disney Pictures, 2007

Re-Animator
Dir. Stuart Gordon
Empire Pictures, 1985

Repo Man
Dir. Alex Cox
Universal Pictures, 1984

The Return of the Secaucus 7
Dir. John Sayles
IFC Films, 1980

sex, lies and videotape
Dir. Steven Soderbergh
RCA/Columbia Pictures Home Video, 1989

Shadows
Dir. John Cassavetes
Lion International Films, 1958

Silence of the Lambs
Dir. Jonathan Demme
Orion Pictures, 1991

S.O.B.
Dir. Blake Edwards
Paramount Pictures, 1981

The Stunt Man
Dir. Richard Rush
Melvin Simon Productions, 1980

Suckers
Dir. Roger Nygard
Blink., 1999

Swingers
Dir. Doug Liman
Miramax, 1996

Titanic
Dir. James Cameron
20th Century Fox, 1997

Tootsie
Dir. Sydney Pollack
Columbia Pictures, 1982

Used Cars
Dir. Robert Zemeckis
Columbia Pictures, 1980

The West Wing
Created by Aaron Sorkin
Warner Bros. Television, 1999-2006

What Happened Was ...
Dir. Tom Noonan
Genre Pictures, 1994

You Can Count on Me
Dir. Kenneth Lonergan
Paramount Classics, 2000

CPSIA information can be obtained
at www.ICGtesting.com
Printed in the USA
BVHW071110150323
660488BV00011B/298